If These WALLS Could TALK:

TORONTO MAPLE LEAFS

Stories from the Toronto Maple Leafs Ice, Locker Room, and Press Box

Lance Hornby

TRIUMPH
BOOKS

Library of Congress Cataloging-in-Publication Data

Names: Hornby, Lance, author.
Title: If these walls could talk: Toronto Maple Leafs : stories from the
     Toronto Maple Leafs ice, locker room, and press box / Lance Hornby.
Description: Chicago, Illinois : Triumph Books LLC, [2019]
Identifiers: LCCN 2019005302 | ISBN 9781629375960
Subjects: LCSH: Toronto Maple Leafs (Hockey team)—Anecdotes. | Toronto
     Maple Leafs (Hockey team)—History.
Classification: LCC GV848.T6 H66 2019 | DDC 796.962/640971354—dc23
     LC record available at https://lccn.loc.gov/2019005302

This book is available in quantity at special discounts for your group or organization. For further information, contact:

Triumph Books LLC
814 North Franklin Street
Chicago, Illinois 60610
(312) 337-0747
www.triumphbooks.com

Printed in U.S.A.

ISBN: 978-1-62937-596-0

Design by Nord Compo

Photos courtesy of AP Images

*To my fellow writers and broadcasters
on the Leafs beat of past, present, and future.
Keep those stories coming.*

CONTENTS

FOREWORD

Playing Saturday on *Hockey Night in Canada* is still the ultimate high for an NHLer. It's even better when you play for the Toronto Maple Leafs. From the instant you wake up that morning, the buzz in the city is palpable. In my era of the 1980s and '90s, by the time you arrived at Maple Leaf Gardens, the atmosphere was unbelievable—no matter how the Leafs were doing or what team was in town. It's still that way at Scotiabank Arena.

When I played minor hockey in the city or as a member of the Niagara Falls Flyers facing the junior Marlies in the afternoon, we'd come to the Gardens early to soak it all in as we watched the Leafs skate in the morning.

The first time I was traded to the Leafs—from the New York Rangers in March 1987—it was a dream come true, but it was also a shocker. We'd played the night before, and I'd had a good game. So when our general manager in New York, Phil Esposito, phoned that morning, I actually thought he might be calling to compliment me. Little did I know, I'd be coming home.

Gord Stellick, later to be my co-host on Leafs radio postgame shows, was the Toronto assistant general manager at the time. He remembers the deal, too. My father had passed away four or five months earlier. My mom was now alone and moving back to Toronto from Vancouver, so it was a nice gesture by both teams to work something out for me to be closer to her.

My first thought before everything sunk in was: *Wow, this is the team I grew up watching.* Right away, it all came back: *Hockey Night,* the sights and smells, the subway rides from the west end with Dad, the College Station stop, the walk down Carlton Street with all the fans—and all the scalpers. I remembered the scent of the popcorn and the chestnuts in the hallways, the ushers with their white hats, and how the bright lights from above accentuated the vivid colours of the seats and playing surface as you emerged from the tunnel and gazed toward the ice. Now I was walking in that same building as a Leaf.

When I took that first step inside the dressing room, all I could think of was how proud my dad would've been and that I wished he could see me play there as a Leaf. There was a sweater hanging with "Osborne" on the back. I'd been traded for Jeff Jackson, so they gave me his No. 12 and just switched the nameplate. I'd already played for two Original Six teams, having been drafted by the Detroit Red Wings, so I considered myself very fortunate to make it three, including my hometown team. But I didn't have a lot of time for nerves—not at 4:30 PM on a gameday.

I don't know if someone can ever be prepared to play for the Leafs. Unlike in Detroit and New York, in Toronto you sense that people know you when you walk around the streets. But you also come to realize what the Leafs were all about for so many decades. They were Canadian boys who did not take that adulation for granted.

At the time I arrived, things hadn't been going too well. There were even draft prospects who'd said they didn't want to play in Toronto. But Wendel Clark had been picked first overall a couple of years earlier and he was changing the views of a lot of people. We played the Pittsburgh Penguins that first game, and it was a great start for me. They had Mario Lemieux, but we played really well and won 7–2. I had a goal, and it was assisted by Russ Courtnall and Todd Gill, who was still with the team when I came back to Toronto a second time in the 1992 trade with the Winnipeg Jets for Lucien DeBlois.

The dressing room is where a team truly grows and the great stories begin. I had the good fortune the first time that coach John Brophy played me with Gary Leeman and Ed Olczyk. The writers called us the GEM line, combining the first initials of our first names, though those two were really the gems, and I was the scuffed-up marble. We had a measure of balance. We were 1-2-3 in team scoring in '87–88, and Leeman scored 50 a couple of years later.

But it was more than just hockey with us because we became close friends off the ice.

Olczyk and Leeman got into horse racing as part owners, and I tagged along. Olczyk and I both got married the same year in 1988. Sure, I was disappointed to be traded in 1990, but at least I went with Olczyk to Winnipeg, and we had a lot of tales about that place, too.

They say timing is everything, and that was certainly the case when I was dealt back to the Leafs two years later. The team was about to turn the corner, even though few players, fans, and media realized it. Pat Burns came in as coach a couple of months after I returned, and we suddenly had that respectability everyone had waited so long for. It was a lot like what's happening with today's Leafs.

Burnsie put me on a line with centre Peter Zezel and fellow winger Bill Berg, and we checked hard, hit hard, and scored a bit. I really enjoyed that role. It became even more special to me that the team as a whole did well, and we almost made it to the Stanley Cup Final in '93.

To have experienced the desolation of the Harold Ballard era when I first arrived, to watching people celebrating and closing down the streets to traffic, that was crazy. I have some great memories and pictures from that time. My wife, Madolyn, and my kids, Abigail and Eliza, tease me that that I'm still riding those stories today. And I'm sure I'll keep telling and re-telling them for years to come. You don't forget anything about being a member of the Toronto Maple Leafs.

—Mark Osborne
Maple Leafs left wing 1986–94

INTRODUCTION

"Hey, you hang around the Maple Leafs? Must have a few good stories, eh?"

Those of us on the beat hear that all the time from fans; while at dinner with friends; via the mailman, the store clerk, or an out-of-town writer curious about Canada's most scrutinized hockey team. I can only reply, "Sure, I have some. How much time do you have?"

It's an intoxicating topic. Once you spin one colourful blue-and-white yarn, you think of another and another with the audience wanting an encore. Often they add their own experiences at the Gardens, involving friends, parents, or grandparents. Maybe they hate the Leafs and have a good tale about a rival getting the last word. For better or worse, to grow up in Toronto is to grow up with the Leafs.

With the Leafs having gone more than 50 years without a title—a challenge fellow authors of the Montreal Canadiens, Dallas Cowboys, and St. Louis Cardinals in the *If These Walls Could Talk* series didn't face, by the way—writing this book meant digging into a trove of older stories from the back files. That's the fun part, as the century-old Toronto franchise is often equal parts history, honour, humour, and human error. Yes, even in championship seasons—13 Stanley Cups from their inception as the Toronto Arenas to their final four in the 1960s—there were still plenty of rough patches. Conversely, their darkest hours produced many light moments.

More than 900 players have suited up for the franchise since 1917, and through many winters, their stories have come to light: a three-team NHL, the construction of the Gardens during the Great Depression, the war years when hockey was a diversion, the good men, the bad apples, the triumphs, and troubled times.

My generation grew up when the Leafs ruled the city. They were on TV every Saturday night before the Blue Jays, Raptors, and *Fortnite*. Though the players were sometimes snowy specs on a tiny black-and-white screen, they seemed larger than life. And the Gardens looked so small from my living room yet so immense when I blinked into its bright lights on my first visit.

My big brother, Mike, took me to see the Boston Bruins-Leafs game on January 7, 1967. We sat in the reds near ice level and we probably dressed up like every patron who attended the Gardens in those days. Toronto won 5–2, and when I recently looked up the summary of that night, Frank Mahovlich opened the scoring from Dave Keon and Ron Ellis, three players I would get to interview extensively in my newspaper years.

As a nervous young reporter in the mid-1980s tentatively taking a seat in the press box for the first time, I took stock of everything around me in case I wasn't allowed back. More than 30 years later, I'm still compiling notes. Hockey as a whole has allowed me to follow the Leafs around the world. I've gone to both sides of the Atlantic for exhibition games and all the way to Asia and the Middle East, where I accompanied alumni in their visits to Canadian troops on peacekeeping missions.

Splitting my time between the Gardens and the Air Canada Centre—recently renamed Scotiabank Arena—I've been to almost 60 arenas where the Leafs have played. My duties at the *Toronto Sun* newspaper have given me great latitude in many stories on the team's past and a chance to interview players going all the way back to their 1932 Stanley Cup team—the first title at the Gardens—to Auston Matthews and the stars of tomorrow. I've been quite fortunate to have a seat on the bus—literally and figuratively—and hope you enjoy this ride.

CHAPTER 1
YOUNG GUNS

Mike Babcock has a term for his young stars, referring to them as "touched by a wand from God." There is no doubting Mitch Marner brings something special to the table every night. The sports term "making something out of nothing" seems the most apt description of the Maple Leafs' top scorer in 2017–18. "What's amazing is most of us have no time and space, whatsoever," Babcock said. "We're banging it here, banging it there, and chasing it. Then the really good guys have all the time in the world, and that's what we're talking about [with Marner]. It seems effortless, and they have the puck all the time, and you can't figure out why. They're just better."

During the 2016 Leafs development camp in Niagara Falls, Ontario, Marner once more crossed paths with Mason Marchment. The then-163-pound Marner found himself looking up at 6'4" Marchment, who two years earlier had received a 10-game OHL suspension for a check to Marner's head, when he was with London, and Marchment was with Erie. "I still tell him he has never said sorry to me," Marner said, laughing.

Marchment, son of former Leafs defenceman Bryan Marchment, claimed he apologized immediately and always maintained it was an accident. Marner was flying past the Erie net after a scoring chance and, while looking away, put himself right in Marchment's path for what the latter argued was a self-defence posture. "Unlucky, really," Marchment said, "I honestly didn't even know I was suspended for it. I was dressed for warm-up the next game, my coach came up and said, 'You're not playing.' I had to watch the video to see why."

Marchment later worked his way into the Leafs with an entry-level contract in 2017.

Marner had a less contentious beginning with Matt Martin. Marner wasn't going to assist on many goals by fourth-line thumper but did help with his marriage proposal. Martin decided the time was right during the spring of 2018 during a Sunday stroll in Toronto's 19th century Distillery District of shops and restaurants.

His longtime girlfriend was Sydney Esiason, daughter of former NFL quarterback Boomer Esiason. Martin's future father-in-law was a huge New York Rangers fan, so there was a somewhat dicey introduction years earlier when Sydney brought home a New York Islander to meet Dad. But the two men eventually got along famously.

Matt got Sydney and their dog, Jax, to pause at an art installation, where hundreds of padlocks were on display by couples to show love and friendship. Matt urged her to take a closer look and while she turned her back he got down on one knee with a ring. Jax got in a few face licks, and a small crowd applauded. Marner shadowed them with a camera and posted the highlights.

*   *   *

One of the first things that new 32-year-old general manager Kyle Dubas did upon replacing Lou Lamoriello in the summer of 2018 was to relax the rules on facial hair. Not only did beards come back in a hurry, but Auston Matthews had the green light to appear in a *GQ* magazine fashion layout, among similar shoots in other publications. He and Marner did a cameo as Cannon Dolls in the *Nutcracker* ballet, and Matthews also appeared on a salty no-holds-barred podcast or two.

Rookies were permitted to do in-game TV interviews, another Lamoriello no-no. "We want them to have interests outside of hockey, to be able to express themselves as individuals," Dubas said. "My philosophy has been: if a person feels they're at their best as an individual, they're going to have their most to give to the team. One of Auston's great interests, outside of the team, is obviously fashion, and it's interesting to see the feedback to *GQ*. Some people are critical, some are thinking, *What is this?* But that's only because it's a non-traditional hobby outside of hockey. If a player golfs, listens to music, or likes a certain type of movie, nothing is ever said. But if it's fashion or something different, such as Garret Sparks likes to DJ...For one it takes a lot of courage [for Matthews] to put yourself in those types of photos. Then you read and you get to know him. I know some people would say, 'Just focus on hockey,' but hockey takes up four hours of their day. There's

20 more hours that we need them to have fulfillment. If it's fashion, clothing, golf, playing *Fortnite*, whatever, as long as they're filling those other hours, and we're helping and encouraging them, I think they'll be better when coming to perform."

For someone dubbed "saviour," Matthews was not on many fans' radar until about a year before the lottery balls lined up for the Leafs. When Toronto made a Christmas trip to western Canada around New Year's 2016 and their last-place finish was starting to take shape, I happened to draw a seat next to a holidaying Marc Crawford, who was then Matthews' coach for Zurich in the Swiss League. "You are not going to believe what this kid can do," said an enthusiastic Crawford, who coached the Colorado Avalanche to the Stanley Cup in 1996 after doing a fine job with Toronto's farm team in St. John's, Newfoundland. "His release, when he lets it go from between the defenceman's legs, using him as the screen, is incredibly quick and deceptive. He's in a league

Auston Matthews pulls on his Maple Leafs sweater after Toronto selects him No. 1 overall in the 2016 draft.

with McDavid and Eichel already. He comes from a good family. Trust me, Toronto is going to fall in love with this kid."

* * *

Within 24 hours of John Tavares' big Canada Day signing with the Maple Leafs, his No. 91 had popped up in the crowd at Blue Jays games, a major betting site moved its needle on Toronto to Stanley Cup favourite, and one car owner proudly drove around town with a JTAVARES vanity license plate. "It was in hopes of him one day coming to Toronto," said real estate manager Tim Parsons, who'd ordered the plate a few years earlier. "I was anxiously awaiting July 1."

Yes, Toronto went J.T. cray-zee after the unrestricted free agent signed. He broke the news by posting a pic of himself asleep in Leafs sheets, and it was widely re-tweeted, indicating he'd chosen home over many NHL suitors. Why wouldn't the city get excited? Star free agents rarely leave their draft teams after nearly a decade when they have prime production years to go. Tavares had been captain of the New York Islanders—their beacon of hope in troubled times on and off the ice—and was counted upon to eventually lead them back to contention in a new arena.

But to choose Toronto, which not long before had been as desirable as Siberia because of its mouldy roster and impatient fanbase, that took a leap of faith. It was a landing padded by a seven-year contract for $77 million, a very good supporting cast, and a Stanley Cup/Olympic champion coach in Mike Babcock.

It was hard for Tavares not to see that adulation heaped on him from the moment general manager Dubas took him on a tour of the dressing room, when he was mobbed at the club's first charity outing of the season, and then training camp in Niagara Falls, Ontario. "It's an adjustment, being in one place as long as I have been," Tavares said. "There is some familiarity from being from here [born in the suburb of Oakville and brought up in nearby Mississauga], but there are still a lot of new things. Plenty of days I've gone out and not been recognized. I've had a lot of attention about people being happy that I'm coming home. That support has been fantastic. [Now it's] just worrying about myself and doing what I have to do to be ready for the season and help contribute. I was very fortunate to be in the position I was in. I just felt the opportunity, the fit to play where I grew up, where I fell in love with the game…you grow up watching them, and that's what you think when you're six or seven years old, [that] you're going to wind up playing for them. I had this once-in-a-lifetime chance."

Tavares had little sleep in the 72 hours leading to the unrestricted free-agency deadline, in which several teams, including the Isles, went hard after him. One of the messages Tavares received during the free-agent interview period was from a young gun Leaf, Matthews, a fellow first overall pick separated by seven years.

Although a small faction of conspiracy theorists wondered if Matthews would have his nose out of joint that he was no longer the clear No. 1 centre and because Tavares' arrival would block his path to being captain, this was no crank phone call. Matthews wanted to reiterate all the things that Tavares heard about the hip young Leafs dressing room with Marner, Morgan Rielly, and William Nylander were true. They needed him. "He's a guy who takes his craft very seriously and he's been one of the premier players since he's been in the league," Matthews said. "We're extremely excited to have John. He makes our team a lot better. It's another step to reaching our ultimate goal."

Halfway through the 2018–19 season, Matthews made his own commitment, a five-year deal for more than $58 million, averaging $11.634 million. The last two digits were a nod to his sweater number. "I hold myself to a higher standard, but in the end, you're measured by championships," Matthews said minutes after the deal was inked. "I love playing here, love my teammates and management top to bottom. There's nothing like playing in this city."

He vowed the money, which made him the highest paid Leafs player ever, would not change his hunger to win. "If I'm making $1 or

$11 million, I'll be the same person every day," he said. "Growing up in Arizona, I never dreamed of playing in a market like this."

Another popular meme soon found its way on the net: the cover of The Beatles' *Abbey Road* album with the heads of Tavares, Matthews, Marner, and Nylander taking the place of Lennon, McCartney, Harrison, and Starr. "You look into trying to build a team that can go far into the playoffs," Dubas said of adding Tavares to his fresh mix of young faces. "We have to get through the first round, get past those two [the Boston Bruins and Tampa Bay Lightning] that finished ahead of us, and stay ahead of all the rest. This was a good way to go about that and perfect that process."

Tavares couldn't wait to get started. "They have accomplished so much in such little time," Tavares said of Matthews and Marner. "You can only think about the trajectory they're on, and that's what gets me excited."

The 2018–19 Leafs did get off to a hot start. Tavares scored in his first game and reached 30 in 48 appearances. He was the fastest Leaf to 30 since Dave Andreychuk in 1993–94 and only the sixth Leafs player with 47 or more in franchise history.

Meanwhile, Marner was among the NHL leaders in points, Rielly led all defencemen for a while, and Matthews began on a near goal-a-game pace. Naturally, the demanding Babcock wanted more. "The team that works the hardest wins most nights," the coach harped. "When you're blessed with a little skill, you might be able to cheat a bit, but in the end, to get what you want in life, your work ethic has to come first. The guy who grinds harder and longer has more fun in the end. It's great that we're fun to watch. I hear that on a nightly basis, but when I hear we're machine-like to watch, I'll be a happy guy."

* * *

In March of 2016, pals Nylander and Kasperi Kapanen were called up by the Leafs after their practice with the Marlies had ended. Elated at the news, but not wishing to make the other feel bad about being ignored, the two sons of NHLers didn't share a text about the good news. "We were kind of quiet," Kapanen said. "But when I saw him in the [Leafs] locker room that night, we started laughing."

A couple of years later, the same two players were trying to get to the Toronto airport when they were rear-ended. Nylander was at the wheel when hit by a female driver. No one, including a passenger in the other vehicle, was hurt. Nylander said the driver knew that the two young men played for the Leafs, though there was little time for chit-chat. After getting the paperwork sorted, the players continued to the airport to make their flight. "Sounds like he did some good driving, so Kappy didn't get hit," Babcock quipped.

The coach related a similar story of Tomas Holmstrom and Nick Lidstrom getting in an accident in Detroit when all were with the Red Wings. "They showed up late for the game, Tommy comes running in my office, and says: 'We had a big accident. But don't worry. When I knew we were going to get hit, I dove in front of [Lidstrom, their star defenceman] so he wouldn't get touched,'" Babcock said.

* * *

Once established on the big team, Marner and Matthews quickly developed a popular post warm-up tradition of flipping a puck or two into the crowd for young kids as they exited for the Leafs locker room. Matthews was shocked one day when an adult intercepted the puck and pocketed it. "I just end up getting another puck and making sure the kid got it," Matthews said. "I've seen that in baseball, too. The older adult steals the ball from the kid. I don't know why that happens. You're an adult, right? You know the feeling, what it's like to be a kid and get a puck or a baseball? I know I was doing the same thing as a kid. Nothing wrong with it. It usually makes their night."

Many who get to the Scotiabank Arena front row at warm-ups bring homemade signs to attract the Leafs' attention for a puck, be it their birthday, first Leafs game, or a road trip from far away. "I like a lot of them, they're pretty clever, they come up with some good stuff," Matthews said.

A sign or two that poke fun at the Leafs star and his post-goal scoring flair is also fine by him. "Some guy made one. It was in Columbus that said, 'Hot Dogs Are A Sandwich' or something like that," Matthews said, laughing. "I thought that was a pretty good one. I was injured, but I saw it on Twitter the next day."

When on the Leafs charter and watching movies, Matthews admits he's a sucker for action movies and the odd romance, though stays away from genres such as horror. Then there's Marner. "He's notorious for watching kid cartoon movies," Matthews said. "I'm not talking *Toy Story* or *Shrek*, but I'll look over, and he's watching *How To Train Your Dragon*."

Matthews said he is a music fan of current rappers such as Drake, Travis Scott, J Cole, and Kanye West, but in the 2017–18 season, he went through a time warp. "I kind of got into the Rolling Stones and older stuff," Matthews said. "You hear their songs, whether it's in movies or commercials. For a big period of time last year, I was listening to old-school stuff."

40 Is the New 20

Patrick Marleau has four kids and not a lot of time during the season to give them his full attention. But he was a hero on nine-year-old Brodie's birthday when he brought him to Leafs practice and let him play a bit in the scrimmage. Marleau's spry condition, nearing 40, led many to joke he might hang on until one of his brood is drafted to the NHL. "That's a long time away," Dad countered.

Babcock thought it was cute that Brodie Facetimed his grandmother in California to show her his personalized practice stall. "A few years from now, we'll dial in on him," the coach promised.

Jon Abbott was the Marlies' broadcaster in the same year the team added Spencer Abbott, a Hamilton-born forward, who was no relation. Spencer had not yet scored for Toronto until the team went on a western Canadian road trip to Abbottsford, British Columbia, to play Calgary's farm team. Sure enough, Abbott scored in Abbotsford with the other Abbott at the microphone. "We had a good chuckle about that," Jon Abbott said. "Then on the flight out of there, when the seats were randomly assigned on the plane, we wound up sitting next to each other."

Jon Abbott's first trip around the AHL circuit required him to get used to the nuances of some very ancient arenas. Oncenter War Memorial Arena in Syracuse, New York, where the hockey classic, *Slap Shot*, was filmed in the mid 1970s, had a tight press box with a steep gangway to enter and leave and a low tilted roof that required occupants to move through like hunchbacks. Safety bars that faced the ice were placed both low and high, making it difficult to either sit or stand to properly call the play unless you watched with your head stuck out between the bars as lanky current Marlies caller Todd Crocker does.

Just before Abbott's first game in one of the AHL's old barns, an elderly arena worker came to his spot in the visitors' radio booth, silently handed him a big American flag, and departed. Abbott eventually figured out it was his job to hold a corner of "The Star-Spangled Banner" during the anthems.

The Marlies differ from their parent team in that they won a Calder Cup in 2018, capping seven straight years in the playoffs with a series record of 12–6. They, too, have had their share of the unusual. In 2015–16 they went through more than 50 players—before any postseason action—and had eight goaltenders win at least one game because of injuries and frequent call-up by the Leafs. One of them was a Zamboni driver they had to recruit on the spot.

Speaking of Zambonis, in 2004 the ice maintenance staff at the Air Canada Centre emulated the Great White Northern custom of burying a $1 loonie coin six inches deep at the faceoff dot at the home of the Leafs, hoping it would pay off with a Canadian win at that year's

World Cup. It was mission accomplished after general manager Wayne Gretzky won Olympic gold in Salt Lake City with a loonie secretly secured beneath its surface. Canada won the World Cup final 3–2 against Finland. "Who says the Canadian dollar isn't strong?" a jubilant Gretzky said. "We're getting a lot of mileage out of this."

Maple Leaf Sports & Entertainment Ltd. chairman Larry Tanenbaum had ordered two specially minted loonies from Ottawa, one for Gretzky and a duplicate for Leafs/Team Canada head coach Pat Quinn. If Quinn buried his coin for Leafs Cup luck, as of 2019, it had not proved powerful enough.

* * *

Wendel Clark's son Kody made a name for himself in 2018, signing an entry-level contract as a second-round pick of the Washington Capitals. But Kody, who surpassed Wendel's dimensions at near 5'7" to a 6'2" right winger with a late growth spurt, was not cut from the same cloth as his father, the team captain, who used fists as well as a wrist shot to make his name. That was evidenced when it took Kody until his third junior year with the Ottawa 67s to get involved in his first fight. "I had 70 by that time," Wendel joked. "He actually did okay [against 6'2" forward Andrew Bruder of the Niagara Ice Dogs]. He was surprised. His hand was sore. I said, 'That's a good sign. If you're just holding on, your hand wouldn't have got sore.' But he doesn't play [1980s] style. The game isn't that anymore. You don't even grow up thinking that anymore. Today it's skating and thinking—at all positions."

CHAPTER 2
THE ORIGINAL LEAFS

Harry Mummery was a 5'11" defenceman whose bulk, estimated between 220 and 240 pounds, made it hard for opponents to get around him when facing the 1917–18 Toronto Blueshirts. In the words of Ottawa's Cy Denneny, "there was a real fear the unstable skating of Mummery would see the big man topple on another player, even a teammate, and do serious harm." On game nights Mummery was wrapped like a mummy into a 12-foot long elastic band by a team trainer that allowed him to squeeze into his equipment.

The Illinois-born, Manitoba-raised Mummery was well known in Quebec, where he'd played pro his first few years, but he made quite an impression in Toronto's first NHL season, starting with his dining habits. He didn't reach that weight missing many meals, and teammate Jack Adams once caught him cooking a huge steak in the Mutual Street Arena boiler room, putting it on the end of a shovel and holding it over the open flame.

Mutual Street, the first home of the Toronto franchise and today a modern apartment block, was located downtown not far from the future Maple Leaf Gardens. The Mutual site also played a part in the city's pro hockey history in the late 19th century. The Caledonian Curling Club stood on the spot, and on February 16, 1888, its members took up the challenge of the neighbouring Granite Curling Club, which had just received delivery of 18 new sticks by rail from Montreal. Under the first coded rules, hockey was already established in Quebec and Eastern Canada by that time, and when a visitor to the Granite Club noticed nothing was organized in Toronto, he ordered the sticks. The Granites, playing on home ice, beat the Caledonians 4–1 in the first recorded game in Toronto.

The Blueshirts of the National Hockey Association were the first ice tenants of Mutual Street on Christmas Day 1912. With a capacity of 7,500, mostly sitting on benches, Mutual had the first artificial ice in Canada east of British Columbia. It housed Toronto's NHA and NHL teams until the late '20s, when its cramped conditions and failure to make a profit sped up plans for a larger home.

As the Gardens was finishing construction in the autumn of 1931, executive Conn Smythe made a one-time offer to any Mutual employee to come over and work at his new building. So many took him up on the chance that maintenance of Mutual's cooling system was left unattended, the ice melted, and the pipes were in such a state of disrepair that another hockey game was never played there. After winning the Stanley Cup in their first year, the Blueshirts were bought by the rink's owners and became known as the Toronto Arenas.

* * *

Blood was thicker than ice, as an Arenas fan found out on February 28, 1920. A fight broke out between Ottawa's Denneny and Cully Wilson of Toronto. While Denneny was sitting on the unsecured penalty bench used in the early NHL, a hot-headed spectator punched him. That didn't sit well with Cy's brother, Corbett, of the Arenas, who jumped in and pummelled the guy.

But family values didn't always work that way. A few years later at the same rink—after the Arenas had been re-branded the St. Patricks—the Toronto-born Conacher brothers, Charlie of the St. Patricks and Lionel of the Montreal Maroons, started a brawl that continued on the common penalty bench.

The St. Patricks struggled at the gate after winning the 1922 Cup, finishing out of the playoffs four of the next five seasons. With buyers circling—including one named Charles Pyle, who was interested in moving the team to Philadelphia—the worry became another strong American-based team would change the makeup of the NHL forever.

J.P. Bickell, a major investor in the club, hoped that a group being formed by local sportsman Smythe could keep the team in town, but Smythe could not raise the reported $200,000 price. Bickell eventually decided to take his $40,000 share and convince fellow St. Pats owners to wait until Smythe could raise the other $160,000. "We paid $165,000 for the St. Pats franchise," Smythe recalled on the team's 50th anniversary in 1977. "It might have been worth $15,000."

Great Nickname

One of the most unusual nicknames bestowed on a Leafs player was Alex "Mine Boy" Levinsky, who never ventured to work below ground in his life. Syracuse-born and a member of the first Leafs team to reside at the Gardens in 1931–32, Levinsky's father did not have full command of English and would shout out while watching young Alex play: "that's mine boy!"

* * *

The Arenas had won a Cup their first season at Mutual Street. But a championship at the Gardens did not seem likely at first, as the Leafs dropped the first game on opening night 2–1 to Chicago and didn't win their first five, which saw coach Art Duncan sacked in favour of Dick Irvin. The first goal in the long history of Gardens was by Chicago's Harold "Mush" March, who had scored the last ever goal at Mutual the season before in an overtime elimination.

But under Irvin the Leafs showed rapid improvement; finished second in the Canadian Division; and defeated Chicago, the Montreal Maroons, and New York Rangers for the title. It was a fun-loving team, whose wild behaviour and pranks included Charlie Conacher once dangling King Clancy from an open hotel window by his feet.

Thrilled at getting the Cup—and beating the Rangers club that fired him a few years earlier—Smythe and Bickell had gold coins imprinted with Bickell's signature, each Leafs player's name, and "Pass as world champion to Maple Leaf Gardens at any time."

In the decades that followed, the fate of those 16 medallions became blurred as hockey treasure hunters and the Hall of Fame sought them from the families or heirs.

In the 2000s Mike Wilson, who had compiled the largest private collection of Leaf artifacts, probably came the closest to getting one of the coveted coins.

A lady from British Columbia contacted me and said she had Busher Jackson's. Her grandfather probably won it in a card game or drinking in a bar as a gift. Her grandfather was born and raised in Winnipeg, where the Leafs had a preseason barnstorming tour in 1934, and Jackson had a five-point game. As Jackson loved to gamble, Wilson and the potential seller were able to piece together that the two card sharks likely settled a poker debt with the pass, though the woman decided to keep it in the end.

Meanwhile, defenceman Fred Robertson had kept his coin from that team in a safety deposit box near his Toronto home. The late season call-up in '32 only played briefly in the NHL, so the coin was a prized possession as he departed the NHL for years of minor league hockey in Cleveland. It was a good thing he chose a bank to hold his treasure as almost all his personal and hockey keepsakes were lost in 1954, when destructive Hurricane Hazel ripped through Toronto and swept part of his house into the Humber River.

The medallion eventually went with him to his retirement home north of the city in Barrie. Those with this golden ticket were urged to come forward in the '70s and '80s when Harold Ballard started messing with Smythe's traditions, usually as a publicity stunt. For example, Cup banners were used as painting tarps, Foster Hewitt's gondola was scrapped, and Ballard made it known that most Leafs stars of the past were unwelcome unless they bought an expensive ticket.

Robertson was urged to show his lifetime passes to embarrass Ballard in a showdown on Carlton Street. "He went with me to the Gardens a few times, but he said, 'We'll just pay,'" his son, Fred Robertson Jr., said. "He never said a bad word about anybody—even Harold. [After his father died], I only brought it to the Gardens once—to show it off rather than try and get in. One of the elderly ushers, who might have been around in '32, studied it, looked at me, and said, 'You don't look that old,' and I had to explain it was my father's, not mine."

Robertson Sr. mostly kept quiet about his place in hockey history. When it came time to customize his memorial stone at Woodland Beach on Georgian Bay, Robertson Jr. was asked if his late father was

31

famous for anything. "I said, 'He won a Cup with the Leafs.' So the guy put a Leafs logo on it that many people in this area remark on."

The Robertsons eventully donated the coin to the Hall of Fame. "It was to be passed down in our family," Robertson Jr. said. "But the people who'd appreciate it most have all died. I have one nephew, but he's not into hockey."

Robertson Sr. was tough on the ice, but he had a chance encounter with one of the meanest men ever to walk the streets. In the early 1940s, he was at a banquet in Cleveland where local celebs were invited, and one of the guests was none other than Al Capone. Though he was in poor health after being paroled, the architect of Chicago's gangland Valentine's Day Massacre in 1929 wound up at the table with Robertson, his wife Marge, and Robertson Jr., who was about four years old. "My father had to get up for a few minutes, and my mother said, 'Please don't leave me alone with Al Capone.'" said Robertson Jr., laughing. "This was some kind of famous fish restaurant, and I ordered a grilled cheese sandwich. Everyone at the table [including Capone] got a laugh out of that, and it's been a family joke since."

* * *

Jack McLean played for the Leafs in the midst of difficult times in World War II and went the extra mile to get his engineering degree at the University of Toronto. It meant he could only play home games in the 1944–45 season. But it seemed his determined efforts would not be rewarded with any fame. Despite the Leafs winning the '45 Cup, he missed the clinching 2–1 game against Detroit with a concussion. And though his name is on the Cup that year, it wasn't until 1948 that rings became a tradition for the winners.

McLean, who never played for another team and became a civil engineer with the Canadian government, was often challenged by doubters in his later years. "You won the Cup? Where's your ring?" was a sneering comment McLean heard so many times.

But in 2002 the Leafs Alumni Association decided it was high time to recognize surviving members who did not have such a bauble. When he heard about the gesture but did not see MacLean's name on the planned list of recipients, Kevin Shea, MacLean's distant cousin and a researcher at the Hockey Hall of Fame, alerted the Alumni Association to the 79-year-old, who was then living in Ottawa. Shea was given the honour of driving there to present a delighted MacLean with his ring. McLean passed away shortly after, and the ring was given to Shea, who wears it to this day.

The Prime Minister's Assistant

Future captain George Armstrong was so young when he first joined the Leafs that his mother had to co-sign his contract. "You felt it was a privilege to sign," said Armstrong, now approaching age 90. "Nine out of 10 rookies got the minimum $7,000, and that's all there was to it." Armstrong could not believe the scene at his first camp as he rubbed shoulders with players he'd only heard of on radio—such as Teeder Kennedy and Max Bentley. He was even assigned to room with Bentley, who asserted veteran provenance on the rookie, getting Armstrong to fetch newspapers and food. "I'd be thankful," Armstrong said of the menial chores. "It was like running errands for the Prime Minister."

Fans with over-active imaginations, such as those in today's social media circles, are not a new phenomenon, especially those favouring the Leafs. Back in Game 2 of the 1956 playoffs, Toronto's Tod Sloan, a cousin of future franchise star Dave Keon, was knocked into the boards by Gordie Howe and suffered a fractured shoulder. Earlier, he'd fought with "Terrible" Ted Lindsay. The Red Wings won both games at the Olympia. In fact, they'd easily beaten the Leafs the previous four times they'd met in playoffs en route to winning four Cups that decade.

So it was likely in part from a sense of frustration that a crank called the *Toronto Star* newspaper several times the next couple of days with a threat to shoot Howe and Lindsay when the series moved back to Toronto. The story was censored for a day so as not to spook the Red Wings until they arrived in Toronto and security could be beefed up. But Howe's mother was quite shaken by the report, and a young Brian Conacher of the famous Leafs hockey clan remembers attending that game and being searched for a weapon at the gate.

But there was more amusement than alarm in the visitors' quarters at the Gardens. *The Globe and Mail* wrote that Red Wings defenceman Bob Goldham hatched a plan to have a trainer sew Lindsay's No. 7 on the front of rookie Cummy Burton and Howe's No. 9 on the back and then push him out on the ice alone for warm-up. The majority of giddy Red Wings backed Goldham's wild idea, but for some reason, Burton wasn't so keen to be served up as a possible sacrifice.

When the game began, Howe and Lindsay combined for three goals in the 5–4 overtime victory. Lindsay's was the winner. Nothing nefarious developed before, during, or after. A grinning Lindsay lingered after the match, circling the ice and pretending to shoot departing patrons with his stick. Sloan later said the Howe hit was accidental, which brought the temperature down the rest of the series.

The man with that master plan, Goldham was from the Toronto suburb of Georgetown and had broken in with the Leafs. He was a member of the amazing 1942 team, which had come back from a 3–0 deficit against the Red Wings in the final—still the only pro sports team in North American sports to pull off that feat in a best-of-seven championship. Those incredible nine days when the Leafs managed to rally saw all manner of motivational tricks. Right before Game 4, coach Hap Day read a letter from a 14-year-old girl, imploring the Leafs not to give up as she was being razzed at school. Leafs officials purposely ripped their team in the media so the Red Wings would get complacent. And the Wings made the mistake of having a giant floral arrangement for a post-Cup celebration on view at the Olympia as the visiting Leafs arrived. All that had as much effect as Day benching some stars to turn club fortunes around, ending in four straight wins and a 3–1 clincher at the Gardens that was witnessed by 16,218, the largest crowd to watch a hockey game in Canada at that time.

In Goldham's later years with the Red Wings, he was victim of elaborate practical joke. His team was in Boston on a road trip when he received a package from his wife, Elly, in Toronto. It contained an old suit that she suggested he wear for good luck. It was tattered with torn seams and the lapel hanging off, but being a good husband, he wore it at the game—much to the derision of his mates. When the Red Wings lost, they blamed the bad karma of Goldham's suit and began tugging at it. Like dead skin, the whole thing—sleeves, legs, and collar—came apart, leaving Goldham in his underwear and the team heading out the door for the train to New York. Just when a cursing Goldham thought he'd have to wear his hockey gear to the station, the Red Wings produced a new suit they'd bought him in Boston.

Another valuable garment was a rare Toronto sweater that turned up in 2013 a long way from the Leafs room. Sudbury's John Arnold was helping to clean out his late grandmother Ila's belongings from a condominium locker. His grandfather was John McCreedy, a member of the famous '42 Leafs Cup team. Arnold thought any remaining prized possessions of his grandfather, who'd died in 1979, were already accounted for and bequeathed to various family members or friends. "I knew of his accomplishments through my grandmother," Arnold said. "He'd died when I was seven, so I just had vague memories. He was just as well-known for being a senior vice president at Inco [the original sponsor of the solid nickel 1976 Canada Cup trophy], but my grandmother kept every single one of his clippings. I read all about this 'speedy young winger from Winnipeg.' When Mom and I went to clean out her locker, she pointed to a box and said I could have anything I found in it. I dug around and saw something curled up in a kitchen-catcher type bag. At first, I thought it was a Canadian flag, but when I rolled it out—oh boy."

It was the No. 14 sweater McCreedy wore with the '42 Leafs and in good condition. NHL sweaters from the war-time era are valued because they were likely a hand-me-down from another player. Clubs could not afford new ones, and with no names on the back, they could be used over the course of a few seasons. "Just a couple of rips and moth holes," Arnold said. "No blood because he wasn't someone who dropped the gloves, but what a find. And to think it almost ended up in the trash."

Before becoming a legend in Boston for guiding the Bruins to a pair of Stanley Cups, Harry Sinden played bantam hockey for the Marlboroughs, the junior affiliate of the Leafs, who began playing at the Gardens from the time the NHL club took residence. Born in the city's Weston neighbourhood that has its own strong hockey tradition, the young Sinden used to take the streetcar downtown, sneak into the Gardens, and hide from security guards to see the Leafs or other clubs practice and play.

Naturally, he had great affinity for his blue and white sweater with its distinctive logo borrowed from the Duke of Marlborough in England. When it came time to turn his into the equipment manager, Percy Topping, Sinden couldn't bear to part with it. "In those days, there were no hockey bags, never mind the modern kind with wheels," Boston scout and Toronto resident Bob Tindall said. "Kids usually jammed all their stuff in the duffel bags their fathers had brought home from serving in the Canadian forces during the war. So Harry took his sweater and put it at the very bottom of his bag with everything else on top. When Topping couldn't find his sweater and accused Harry of taking it, Harry grabbed the bag from the end—careful to hold the sweater—and shook all his equipment out on the floor and said, 'Told ya, it ain't here.'"

* * *

In 2018 the City of Toronto finally got around to honouring a Toronto-born captain of the Leafs. Sid Smith, whom son Blaine celebrated as a true man of the people, had an outdoor rink named after him at Christie Pits, a place where he played shinny as a boy and often popped by to play with fans in the 1950s. Sid passed away in 2004. "Dad would tell stories about coming home from Leafs practice and just taking his skates and stick out to play shinny with the local kids," Blaine said. "That was my father. He didn't think of himself as anyone special just because he played for the Leafs. It would be something my dad would be proud of—as a Torontonian. He was the only local guy on the team at one point. Everyone else was from out West or up North."

Beginning in 1946–47, Smith played left wing and was part of three Toronto Cups—two in the late 1940s—including '49, in which he played one regular-season game but scored five goals in the playoffs. As part of those five goals, he had a Game 2 hat trick in a sweep of the final against Detroit. Between the retirement of the great Teeder Kennedy and the naming of George Armstrong in the next decade, Smith served as captain for 1955–56, relinquishing the "C" upon Kennedy's brief return.

*   *   *

For the first generation of fans on *Hockey Night in Canada*, Murray Westgate seemed as real as the Leafs on their flickering black-and-white televisions. Westgate was the face of Esso gasoline, a major sponsor of *Hockey Night*, and he wore a service station suit complete with hat and bow tie. When he wasn't pitching motor oil or unveiling the first cumbersome credit card machine to pay at the pumps, he sat in on the *Hot Stove League*, the intermission feature with a real pot-bellied stove and a panel of writers and retired Leafs such as Charlie Conacher.

Jingles such as "Happy Motoring" and the catchphrase "put a tiger in your tank" became staples from 1952, when the show went on air, until 1968 when Esso—and Westgate—were moved out. "As a kid watching *HNIC*, I really did believe he had his own Esso station," said hockey historian Paul Patskou. "And I believe that people from out of town drove around looking for Murray's station in Toronto."

The Regina-born Westgate, a radio operator in the Canadian Navy during the Battle of the Atlantic in World War II, lived to be 100 before passing away in 2018. A famous story had Westgate hanging by the players' bench at the Gardens in his station attire after shooting an

Esso ad before a Toronto-Detroit game. As Howe and the Red Wings came off the ice, Mr. Hockey pointed out Westgate to teammates and said, "there's the guy with the best job in the league."

* * *

Before Punch Imlach arrived on the scene to start a run of four championships, the general manager was Howie Meeker. He won a Cup as a player and still holds the NHL rookie record for five goals in a game on January 8, 1947. But with Meeker as their coach, the Leafs missed the playoffs in 1956–57. Meeker was then moved to GM but got under Conn Smythe's skin right away by expediting the signing of rookie Frank Mahovlich and extolling his strengths to members of the press. Smythe had preferred letting the kid sweat out the negotiations and take a discount. "The [Mahovlich signing] hit the newspaper, and I don't think it was on the street a half hour before Smythe was on the phone," Meeker said at the time. "He was steaming mad and tore a strip off of my back. He said, 'You're saying all these complimentary things about this young kid, and that's going to cost us money. You can't say anything at all—how bad you want him, how good he is, or anything. Just shut up.'"

Meeker did not get much chance to run anything his way, as Conn's son, Stafford, was also emerging as a powerful figure at the Gardens. Meeker was fired after five months as GM but did get the last word with the younger Smythe when the two men had an office showdown.

"We got nose-to-nose," Meeker told the *Toronto Star*'s Kevin McGran nearly 50 years later. "He gave me a shove, and I hit him between the [bleeping] eyes."

CHAPTER 3
THE FINAL CUP ERA

Dickie Moore is most famous as a member of the Montreal Canadiens' dynasty. But in his short stint as a Leafs player in 1964–65, he was shocked to look across the Toronto room between periods of a playoff game and see three-time Leafs champions, Tim Horton and Red Kelly, leaning on each other's shoulders—fast asleep. That scene typified the laid-back approach many Leafs had at the time despite Punch Imlach being a relentless coach. "Just resting my eyes," Kelly insisted.

But there had been an earlier episode—this time involving the police—when both Horton and Kelly were unquestionably wide awake. It was training camp in 1963 after a road exhibition game against the senior Quebec City Aces. Horton, Kelly, and a few Leafs were walking down a road in the provincial capital that was under construction and lined with concrete barrels. Some of the Leafs playfully attempted to knock over the heavy cylinders, daring the brawny Horton to try himself. Not only did Horton push one to the ground, but it also went careening down a hill like a boulder in a cartoon. It didn't hit anyone or cause damage. However, witnesses called the cops, who attempted to get Horton in their squad car. "But Tim's got a grip on each side of the open door," Kelly, who passed away in May of 2019, wrote in *The Red Kelly Story*. "Of course, with his strength they can't budge him. One of the cops took his billy club and whacked him in the hand. He let go and they shoved him in. He spent that night in jail. Punch found out and went down the next morning, cleared it up, and got him out because we had to fly to Montreal. It was some hijinks."

* * *

Bert Olmstead played for the Leafs in the late '50s and early '60s and was on the first of three Cup champions. In the playoffs the year before, the left winger was subject to a radical injury treatment as he tried to get back in the semifinal series against the Detroit Red Wings despite having one eye swollen shut. Leafs physiotherapist Karl Elieff, one of the first of his profession in the NHL, had attended a National Trainers Association seminar in Gainesville, Florida, where they met a colleague who'd experimented with live leeches to reduce the effects of a hematoma.

Olmstead would not relent to urges he take himself out of the lineup, so Elieff and trainer Bob Haggert, who had been at the same sports medicine conference, decided to try the leeching method. They grabbed a cab, went to a local chemist's shop, and came back with a leech they named Larry. Olmstead was so determined to get back that he was willing to try whatever the staff was proposing, so he sat still while Larry was placed on his eyelid and did his thing. Players and staffers, who came in the medical room and saw Olmstead, were grossed out, but soon he felt better, and his vision improved.

Now Elieff and Haggert had another problem—how to get the leech detached from Olmstead. After much debate they just tore Larry away, causing a little bleeding, but Olmstead didn't care. Later, they were informed that a lit cigarette held near Larry would've have caused him to let go.

* * *

George Armstrong always played down fabled tales involving himself, but teammates told and re-told them enough that they must be included here—even if full details never came out. The first had to do with his late, great teammate Johnny Bower. Knowing the uber-polite goalie was always on his best behaviour around women in public, the mischievous Armstrong invited him out one afternoon on the road to a major department store on the pretext of buying their wives a purse or scarf.

Armstrong kept leading Bower deeper and deeper into the ladies' section to a discreet aisle with intimate apparel. He then told Bower to wait a moment, telling him he was going to the washroom—and then giddily watched from afar as the nervous Bower stood uncomfortably next to all the gaudy bras and panties for almost a half hour while suspicious and frowning females passed him by.

That wasn't the only prank Armstrong pulled on Bower. After a practice one day, Bower came off the ice and reached for the case holding his dentures above his locker. His real teeth had been long lost to the hockey wars of the pre-mask era. He kept trying to pop the dentures into place without success until he noticed the smirking going on around him and realized they weren't his chompers. Bower suspected Eddie "The Entertainer" Shack was behind the shenanigans, but Armstrong eventually fessed up, further riling up Bower by telling him he got the false teeth from a mortician.

Armstrong played a club-record 1,187 games and in his later years began to enjoy the benefits of the sauna. But he also liked his privacy in there and was angered one day when a number of Leafs crowded into the communal steam room. He was said to have solved that problem by urinating on the heated stones, causing a stench that cleared the place out in a flash. However, the angry sauna attendant demanded Armstrong pay to replace the soiled specialty stones.

When he found out how much they cost, the frugal Armstrong decided to do it on the cheap. He took his car to an unobserved bank of the Don River and loaded it with similar-looking stones that were randomly scattered about. He dropped them off at the sauna, complaining all the while to the attendant about the high price and the effort involved in restoring them. Later, when the other Leafs had gathered for a good sweat, Armstrong's water-logged rocks began exploding in the high temperatures, causing a frantic evacuation.

On the much colder ice, Armstrong's empty net goal to clinch the '67 Cup has been replayed so many times that some people assume it was the game winner back on May 2, 1967. But that honour, as Armstrong tries to remind those who keep slathering him with nostalgic praise, belongs to Jim Pappin, who was also the league's leading playoff scorer that year.

Pappin's go-ahead goal in the 3–1 final came at the 19:24 mark of the second period on a backhand pass attempt to teammate Peter Stemkowski that glanced off the skate of Canadiens defenceman Jacques Laperriere. It was originally credited to Stemkowski, who in sportsmanlike fashion went to the officials to make sure they got the scoring sequence correct.

The '67 Cup is still perfectly preserved in everyone's mind from that era—not just because it was Toronto's last to date, came against

Montreal, or that the average age of the players on the club was around 32.

It was for the achievement despite the long odds. At midseason Toronto dropped 10 straight (the pre-shootout record) and seemed headed for play-off race elimination—never mind the title. The slump had an adverse effect on Imlach's already strained relations with some players and certainly his health. After a morning pregame pep talk before a game against the Boston Bruins, he began suffering chest pains and was advised to go to hospital.

It wasn't a heart attack as many feared, but a case of exhaustion, which prompted assistant general manager King Clancy to go behind the bench. The Leafs were already coming out of their skid, but with the colourful Irishman in charge, the mentally relaxed players found their groove and went undefeated in another six as Imlach's condition gradually improved. "A team is like a musical instrument," wrote Frank Mahovlich in *The Big M*. "You tune it up, and it's as good as it gets. If you tighten it, it will break. And that's what happened to us. We broke. So in comes Clancy and he was the opposite to Imlach. He just let the reins go. Everybody did what came naturally."

* * *

Imlach's superstitions were too numerous to list. But when he got other people entangled trying to circumvent the fates, chaos often ensued. That often involved Haggert, who was a frequent road companion when the players were out on the town. For a good 10 years or so, Haggert had to put up with Imlach looking for lucky pennies and shamrocks and disposing of any Canadian $2 bills that appeared in loose change. When fans found out about Imlach's obsessions, people sent him rabbit's feet, and some women dropped off their lucky bras. It was Haggert's job to catalogue and store all the bizarre items.

Before games, Imlach made sure he and Haggert were the last to leave the room, and Imlach would tap the sticks of No. 7 (Horton) and whichever Leafs player wore 11 at the time. The worst for Haggert was when Imlach insisted they go to the movies, where the boss demanded they sit 11 rows down and seven seats in. If that valued seat was occupied, Imlach would ask Haggert or Clancy to get the person to move. When they wouldn't— and a few fights almost resulted—Imlach would just go to another theatre.

Haggert was there during all the Cups and became a pioneer in the business of sports licensing, playing a business role in the 1972 Summit Series against the Russians. Haggert's grandmother worked at the Gardens in the restaurant that was part of the first era, and she helped him land a job as a stick boy with the junior Marlboroughs in 1949. It was Haggert who taped up Bobby Baun's fractured ankle in the '64 playoffs so the defence-man could get back in the game for an overtime goal against Detroit.

Prior to the '67 Cup final against the Habs, Imlach was at the top of his motivational machinations, and it was driving Montreal rival Toe Blake nuts. Imlach ordered new sweaters with a Canadian Confederation-style Leaf on the front (it was the nation's centennial year) and showed films of the Leafs' three previous Cup parades for the benefit of the youngsters.

Imlach paid a visit to his favorite Montreal tailor before the series and ordered a new green-checked jacket, advising the store's owner that he intended to look good on colour TV the night the Leafs would win the Cup. Imlach indeed wore it for the Game 6 clincher.

When the Leafs lost Game 4, Imlach cut out the pictures of the Habs celebrating and posted them around the dressing room, telling his men, "A picture's worth a thousand words, isn't it?" Before Game 5 in Montreal, he supposedly dumped a box of large bills in the middle of the room, declaring, "This is what it's all about" and walked out. The Leafs won 4–1. He also had an aversion to playing postseason games on Thursdays. The Leafs record was 0–4 vs. the Chicago Blackhawks and Habs on Thursdays that April, and had the Leafs not won Game 6, the deciding match would've been Thursday, May 4.

More than 20 years later when Imlach had his second coming as general manager, not much had changed. He ordered Gord Stellick, his executive assistant, to go down to the massive Gardens vault and break some $100 bills into smaller notes. "I assumed he'd want a mix of everything," Stellick said. "So, I got him 20s, 10s, 5s, and a couple of smaller ones. I put them on his desk, but he immediately and sternly raised his voice and told me to pick up the $2 bills—I think there were only two of them—and get them out of his sight."

*   *   *

To many fans across the generations, Mahovlich was the quintessential Maple Leaf. The Big M was a graceful winger, prolific scorer, good Northern Ontario boy, and a graduate of local hockey power St. Michael's College. Dave Keon, who came to St. Mike's a couple of years later, humourously recalled Mahovlich was the golden boy on campus. If they arrived late for a class because of hockey, the priest/instructors would give Mahovlich a morning greeting, compliment his play in a recent game, and then turn to Keon and admonish him for being tardy.

After four Cups and a flirtation with 50 goals, Mahovlich was eventually traded to Detroit and on to archrival Montreal, where he won two more Cups in 1971 and '73. He was still spry enough to want to play in Toronto in his mid-30s. But it wasn't the Leafs who lured him, as he joined the World Hockey Association's Toronto Toros.

Forming a nucleus of ex-Leafs and Toronto Marlie juniors who couldn't get Leafs owner Harold Ballard to pay them market value, the Toros felt right at home in the rented Gardens.

For Mahovlich, who'd just departed the Habs after a 31-goal season and a glorious NHL career, playing with a few lesser lights on the Toros took some getting used to. After a few games, he turned to his young linemate Gavin Kirk and said in jest, "You're the worst centre I've ever played with."

Kirk was hurt and angered by the comment, so the fun-loving Mahovlich kept up the chirping: "Finally, Gavin's had enough of my teasing and says, 'Okay, so who'd you play with before me?' I said, 'Well, there's Dave Keon, Alex Delvecchio, and Jean Beliveau [all three Hall of Famers]. Gavin thought for a second and said, 'Okay, it's not a bad list to be fourth on."

45

Born in Timmins, Ontario, Frank Mahovlich represents the quintessential Maple Leafs player to many Toronto fans.

Kirk worked for Molson's Brewery for 30 years. "At my retirement party, I received a note from Mahovlich," Kirk said about the player who would become a member of the Canadian Senate. "It read, 'Congratulations on such dedication and commitment in your life. And P.S.: you're still the worst centre I've ever played with.'"

* * *

How did the Leafs go south so fast after their 1967 Cup? It started just weeks after they beat the Canadiens. Montreal general manager Sam Pollock had the upper hand for the June 6 expansion draft, and no one else in the NHL raised much fuss that he was allowed to write some of the draft rules. Imlach, meanwhile, did not or would not take the needed precautions about his personnel.

The Leafs' draft day losses included goalies Terry Sawchuk and Gary Smith, defencemen Bob Baun and Al Arbour, and forwards Larry Jeffrey and "Cowboy" Bill Flett. Not only were they gone, but they also weren't replaced on the fill-in list with NHL-bound players as the other Original Six clubs made sure to do. Imlach was too concerned about a clause in Toronto's recent deal involving minor league players on the Rochester farm team. He transferred many farmhands without realistic NHL futures to the protected list to save a potential $30,000 if any were taken in the expansion draft.

That frugality made other NHL caliber players such as Eddie Joyal, Mike Corrigan, Darryl Edestrand, and Lowell McDonald available to other teams as the draft went on. Coupled with the sale of the Leafs' Western Hockey League pro team in Victoria, B.C., for profit, it was a loss of depth the Leafs would truly feel a few years later when the WHA raids began.

In addition to Baun's departure to the Oakland Seals, the Leafs had an unhappy Larry Hillman to deal with. After playing a vital role in the Cup victory, the veteran defenceman wanted his pay bumped from $15,000 to $20,000, a raise which Imlach staunchly refused. It became a stand-off many teammates watched closely as a test case for their own contracts.

For more than three weeks, Hillman held out and was fined $100 a day. He eventually gave in after $2,400 was forfeited, but unlike other instances when the player would eventually recoup the cash after harmony was restored, he is still waiting for the money—with interest.

Hillman famously put a Cup curse on the Leafs, though he claimed to have lifted it after it reached 50 years in 2017. On the ice Hillman was never the same dedicated player after the dispute and soon departed. Many Leafs also felt the club betrayed him and made their own plans to leave at the first contractual opportunity.

Still feeling good about winning the '67 Cup against the odds, Imlach was not too worried about the long-range state of the team until an exhibition game the following autumn against the New York Rangers. After Pete Stemkowski laid out a couple of Rangers with clean hits, he was jumped in retaliation, and no Leafs came to his aid in the ensuing brawl. "Any time four guys from one team have enough free time to have a vendetta with one guy from another, that second team is in trouble," Imlach wrote in *Heaven and Hell in the NHL*. "And I should have seen it. I should have known right then. I should have taken them straight into the dressing room and said, 'Okay, we'll straighten this out right now.' I should have pointed out to them that there were too many guys backing up. We won the game 4–3, but it was like winning the battle and losing the war."

Around the same time, more Leafs were getting involved in the newly formed NHL Players Association and its firebrand leader, Alan Eagleson. Toronto's Bob Pulford was selected to head the new union but quickly found himself replaced on the Leafs' top line by Imlach, who loathed Eagleson. Later in the season, Mahovlich's mentally draining battle of wills with Imlach, which had dragged on the whole decade, caused him to briefly leave the team. Mahovlich was also in the union camp, and the rift reached a point where an angry Imlach ran a practice with the team divided into perceived rebels and loyalists. As Toronto was fading from the playoff race, Imlach traded The Big M to Detroit in a seven-player deal, which not only marked the end of the Leaf dynasty, but also broke the hearts of many fans.

CHAPTER 4
MEDIA MADNESS

The first beat reporters to follow the Leafs around had a much more chummy relationship with management, coaches, and the players. Newspapers were the sole outlet covering the show and were the only media who travelled with the club and shared some of their late-night antics. Players and media used to run into each other in the same restaurants and bars.

But fans with a proclivity to using social media, especially for darker purposes, virtually killed off the custom of players going to most public establishments. Sometimes, however, the fourth period still finds the fourth estate and players sharing a drink. At one road stop on the evening before a meaningless regular season game, the only available late-night haunt was subdivided into a strip bar. A media person dropped in on the tamer side but spotted several Leafs, including both goalies, enjoying the $5 ballet with no sign of leaving soon. The guy decided it was best he move on without giving the impression he was shadowing the players but not before calling a bookie and betting heavily against the Leafs in the next evening's game. The Leafs not only lost, but they also lost badly.

Back in the day, though, most ink-stained wretches found favour with the higher-ups and manager Conn Smythe. So they played along when Smythe was anxious to knock the champion Toronto Argonauts off the front pages in the autumn of 1949. With the Grey Cup party still in full swing around town, Smythe announced he intended to bench rollie pollie All-Star goalie Turk Broda if he didn't drop seven pounds. Broda's "Battle of the Bulge" captivated the city going forward. There were pictures of the goalie eating healthy food, getting weighed on a giant scale, or running through the streets to shed fat while children cheered him on. Smythe didn't just spotlight Broda for his campaign. He berated skaters Howie Meeker, Vic Lynn, and a couple of others for being out of shape, even though this was the team in the midst of winning three straight cups. "I'm not running a fat man's club," Smythe told reporters despite the fact the Leafs had just won the Cup.

Meeker said he and Lynn were bitter about Smythe's ploy for a long time after.

"We disliked the guy, but he certainly got our attention—and the media's," Meeker said.

For some newsmen a yearly gift from Smythe was in the form of a Christmas bonus such as a TV set. But when new *Toronto Star* sports editor Milt Dunnell was given $250 at holiday time, he turned it over to the paper's children's charity. Smythe was puzzled at Dunnell's not taking the cash himself but eventually accepted this new arrangement. Smythe was careful to keep the story from George McCullagh, a Maple Leaf Gardens director and owner of the rival newspaper, *The Globe and Mail*, who wouldn't have approved of a rival paper getting Gardens money for any purpose.

* * *

For fans following the Maple Leafs games at home in the 1960s, there was a cozy comfort zone of Foster Hewitt on radio, son Bill on TV, and the latter's analyst, Brian McFarlane. But games against the Montreal Canadiens at the Forum were strange experiences as the CBC opted for the local broadcast team of Danny Gallivan and Dick Irvin.

Irvin's father, Dick Sr., was coach of the Leafs between 1931–32 (the year of Toronto's first Cup at the newly opened Gardens) and 1940. Irvin Jr. grew up admiring Foster, the first voice of the Leafs and a radio icon. But when Irvin Jr. began work in Montreal, he found it "disappointing" that the elder Hewitt could never remember who he was. "Despite his long association with Dick Sr., he never mentioned him to me," Irvin wrote in *My 26 Stanley Cups*. "When we met I would always re-introduce myself and lean on the name 'Irvin,' but it didn't work, and he never once called me by name. I was always 'kid.' Obviously, my first broadcasting hero wasn't interested, or more to the point, I guess, wasn't impressed. Maybe he'd had a falling out with Dick Sr. [who later worked in Montreal]."

Irvin Jr. and Bill Hewitt did have some rapport and even worked a few special assignments before Bill's passing in 1996. Irvin Jr. picked up on some of the same idiosyncrasies that McFarlane noted through the years. With little or no warning—sometimes in the middle of the analyst's comment—Hewitt would slap his colour man on the back and then shake hands, a way to give some reassurance for himself that the broadcast was going well. "The first couple of times he did it to me it was quite a jolt," Irvin Jr. recalled. "I learned to brace myself from then on."

McFarlane had become quite used to Hewitt's unusual habit. "Bill was such a nice man and tried to make me feel at home by patting me very hard on the back," McFarlane said. "So I'd end up saying, 'K-K-Keon has the puck' as I was being pushed forward so far—right into the mic."

McFarlane enjoyed his celebrity but not while making the precarious climb down from the Gardens gondola catwalk after the game. He had to get back to ice level as soon as possible to interview one or more of the three stars. "They didn't like the post and pregame walk-and-crawl to get down from there," he said, "at least before they put in handrails."

Seeing McFarlane was also a chance for a few peanut gallery critics to unload. "I wore the famous blue *Hockey Night in Canada* jacket, and you'd be hoping there'd be no stoppage in play so you wouldn't get recognized," McFarlane said. "While I was up there, people would be yelling, 'Jump McFarlane, jump' or tell [colleague] Gary Dornhoeffer to do the same. One night a guy notices me on the way down and yells, 'Hey McFarlane, you're the reason I come here to watch the games. I can't stand you on TV.'"

While McFarlane wore the blue Hockey Night jacket, Joe Bowen, who has been lucky enough to work games in the Gardens and the ACC/Scotiabank Arena, detested the loud sports jackets that he and Harry Neale sported in the Global TV days. "Harry and I had these horse blankets they made us wear. They were so heavy and a God-awful colour. We just hated them. At the end of one year, the last game night, our producer, Mark Askin, told us, 'good news guys, you can go back to wearing nice light suits next season.' So, Harry and I were sitting up there when everyone had left the Gardens, and Harry happily hurls his jacket out of the press box. You could see it wafting down through to the red seats. Then I tossed mine, too. We had a good laugh about it. A few minutes later, an arena cleaner guy comes running up to us, panting heavily, and says, 'Mr. Bowen, Mr. Neale, here, you dropped your jackets.'"

Foster Hewitt, notably, did no pregame research for his hundreds of radio broadcasts—at least that anyone remembers. He would walk in from the street near game time, be handed a lineup with scratches, and take it from there. Bowen, though, liked to be a lot more prepared. "Before the Internet it was an adventure," Bowen said. "You had to get your own notes, do your research, compile your interviews. Now, so much can be done at home on the net."

When the broadcast crew travelled with the team, they were able to get some story nuggets for the game by interacting with the players. But travelling with the Leafs even for rights holders was discouraged under the 21st century Lamoriello-Dubas regimes. Bowen, Jim Ralph, TV host Paul Hendrick, and producer Nicole Burns all fly commercial with the other media.

At the same time, newspaper ranks have dwindled across the NHL, especially on the road as travel budgets and ad revenues decrease. But the Leafs—whether at Scotiabank Arena or on the road—are still a story attracting lots of TV, radio, bloggers, wire services, special publications, and still a fair amount of writers. "When I started," Bowen said, "there would be four or five writers: John Iaboni, George Gross, Frank Orr, Bill Houston, Rick Faser, and some radio people... Now, you go to Leaf practice and there are about 40 people and lots of cameras."

* * *

In the early '90s, new general manager Cliff Fletcher endeared himself to the media right away in the simplest of gestures. If a big trade or significant move was imminent and would be taking place after practice or an off day, he'd mention to beat reporters, "Stay near a phone." This was obviously prior to the Internet era. By giving journalists a heads-up, it meant scribes didn't waste too much time with secondary stories, and deskmen at their papers weren't tearing out their page layouts up at the 11th hour.

However, in the Gardens' informal atmosphere, everyone—from the Zamboni driver to the little old lady selling popcorn in the greys—seemed to know every move the hockey team made within minutes. Bartenders near the Gardens also became the first to get the scoop on something—if any office personnel happened to drop in.

But by the time Pat Quinn, Brian Burke, Dave Nonis, Lou Lamoriello, and Kyle Dubas were in charge, there was an information vacuum. Routine news was difficult to receive or deliberately announced at the most inopportune time. In the Burke era, coach Ron Wilson tweeting his contract extension on Christmas Day morning was the low point. Despite dozens of reporters in the building who could have given the team maximum publicity for the Luke Schenn-James van Riemsdyk trade at the 2012 draft in Pittsburgh, Burke gave no alert of its impending conclusion. Leafs scouts had already recapped their selections to reporters, and above the Consul Energy Centre's private boxes, the Leafs and other teams were busy hosting their drafted player and their families for a reception. The *Toronto Star*'s Kevin McGran and myself had the most deadline work to do and were among the last to exit the draft floor work area while impatient arena workers hovered over, ready to dismantle our table and prepare the rink for a concert. Relieved to be done and aiming to be back in Toronto around 10:00 PM, we hopped in his car. Burke, however was already confiding to Leafs TV and everyone else in the suite that he'd pulled the trigger on the trade. About 45 minutes on the highway north of Pittsburgh, our cell phones lit up with the official trade release.

Swearing profusely, we discussed driving back to town and re-booking our rooms, maybe hunting down Burke for quotes, but the Leafs rushed the conference call with van Riemsdyk. With no place to turn off the road, McGran and I rigged our phones so one could dial into the call and ask questions while the other recorded. The result was McGran trying to hold his phone and the steering wheel as we weaved across our lane on Interstate 79. In the midst of one Q & A exchange with van Riemsdyk, the audience could hear McGran's interaction with a toll booth officer about getting a receipt.

* * *

Under normal circumstances, writers want fast games, though woe to the man or woman in the press box who blithely mentions how quickly a game is progressing. The cursed comment will surely be followed by extra innings, overtime, shootout, or some other unforeseen calamity. But one blustery evening in the late '90s, *Toronto Star* colleague Paul Hunter and I were openly cheering for a Leafs road game at old Nassau Coliseum on Long Island to drag on as long as possible. The reason? We weren't yet there, having missed the morning skate, the warm-up, and possibly the entire game.

Since 7:00 AM we'd been stuck at Pearson Airport as flight after flight from Toronto to LaGuardia and Newark, New Jersey, was canceled because of unusually high winds along the Eastern seaboard. As both of us were new dads at the time, we tended to choose early gameday flights rather than traveling the day before so that we could apply the extra time at home. We figured short hops such as New York, Boston, and Pittsburgh were worth the gameday flight risk.

But this time the real fear was that we'd actually miss a game, an inconvenience our bosses wouldn't like, and, perhaps worst of all, we'd get jeered by our comrades and the Leafs. By late afternoon it was too late to rent a car, though two of the four NHL officials with us at Pearson, who were scheduled to work the same game, had decided to fly to the open airport in Philadelphia at 5:00 PM and drive the rest of the way to Nassau Coliseum.

Paul and I weighed the same plan, but a flight to LaGuardia finally was cleared for 6:00 PM, about an hour before game time. We landed, rushed through the LaGuardia terminal to the first taxi we saw, and asked the driver to burn rubber—and find the Isles' broadcast on radio. We pulled out our computers and tried to catch up with both pregame notes and as much running copy as possible on the 45-minute journey to the Coliseum.

We burst into Nassau's cramped press box late in the middle frame, squeezing past surprised radio man Bowen with our suitcases. We'd arrived smack in the midst of frenzied end-to-end action—almost in tandem with our two zebra pals, who'd done their Philly-to-Uniondale car rally, quickly dressed, and hopped over the boards to join their brethren. As he tried to keep up with the scoring chances and the sudden appearance of the two missing officials, Bowen also found time to chirp the late arrival of us writers. Paul and I cobbled together enough of a story that made sense for our papers and grabbed a quick beer before departing at 5:00 AM for our return flight.

* * *

Wendel Clark, who celebrates a goal against the Los Angeles Kings in 1993, generated a lot of consideration for the 1986 Rookie of the Year.

Wendel Clark's offensive numbers in the club's push to get him the Calder Trophy weren't exactly record-setting, but he did get a kind of record out of it. Clark was a hot commodity in Toronto, generating much Rookie of the Year talk in Toronto and elsewhere in 1986. "I had a friend from high school, Bob McAlpine, who had a band called Cats Can't Fly. Their claim to fame was they opened for Tears For Fears on their six-date Canadian tour, but no one from Tears For Fears ever deigned to speak to them the entire time," said Bob Stellick, the Leafs' business director. "Anyway, McAlpine says he's written this song, 'Clark for Calder' with the hook: 'the choice is clear, rookie of the year.' Harold Ballard heard about it and liked the idea. So they went ahead recording it. Afterward, it was like that scene from *Coal Miner's Daughter* [with] us pressing records and mailing them all over the place."

Clark had the publicity machine rolling and scored 34 goals that season, but there was a strong anti-Ballard sentiment at the time that Stellick sensed. The boss had just ticked off too many people for too many years with his insensitive comments, attacks on the league, restrictive media policies, and his general buffoonery. "We tried to overcome the anti-Harold thing," Stellick said. "Up to Christmas we were up against Kjell Dahlin of the Canadiens, and Wendel was having a great year. Then he fell off, and we lost to Calgary's Gary Suter. Wendel also had some drawbacks, just 11 assists and a really ugly, ugly plus/minus."

Stellick pointed out that the Maple Leafs got some more positive publicity the next decade. The Leafs were still profitable and a great story in 1993, even though the Toronto Blue Jays were a World Series club at the time. "After our amazing run that year, Mark Askin, our game night producer with Molstar, told me, 'We're thinking of a highlight video. Can we do a deal?' I thought sure. We'd never really had any highlight reels for a long while when we were losing in the '80s. It had been more like one projector slide. So we did this package called 'The Passion Returns.' Mark thought it would sell 25,000 copies; it ended up being about 300,000."

* * *

Jiggs McDonald, who handled Leaf broadcasts from 1995–98, laments the end of media informality in the 21st century NHL. "There used to be a fantastic relationship between players, broadcasters, and writers. You could just go up to a guy and start talking about anything. But now it's, 'Oh, did someone from [media relations] know you were going to speak to a player?' Now you have to go through someone to talk to someone. There's a sense of entitlement now among some players that they don't have that obligation to speak. But I still hear a lot of American reporters say, 'Thank God football is over, and I can talk to hockey players again.' The driving force in most dressing rooms is Canadian kids from middle class families, who have their feet on the ground, who are accessible and well-spoken."

McDonald came away with a nice scoop for his radio station, Orillia's CFOR, in the summer of 1967. Before being officially hired by the expansion Los Angeles Kings as their radio voice, McDonald was in Toronto, completing his job interview with the club's bombastic owner, Jack Kent Cooke. Hogtown was Cooke's base, where he had media properties and previously owned the Toronto Maple Leafs Triple A baseball team.

McDonald spotted Leafs great Red Kelly coming out of Cooke's suite with Kings GM Larry Regan. McDonald became aware of a secret plan that Kelly would announce his retirement after he'd just helped Toronto win the Cup and then become the Kings' first coach. It would all be unveiled at the coming expansion draft in Montreal.

But Leafs management—Punch Imlach and Stafford Smythe—were not about to lose Kelly for nothing when they found out the Kings' intentions. As the draft unfolded, they protected Kelly in hopes of forcing the Kings to trade an asset for his freedom. As the Kelly episode came to a head, McDonald was told by Cooke to find Imlach and Smythe and bring them to his office. McDonald wound up helping referee the profanity-laced dispute. Eventually, Kelly was allowed to go to L.A., while Toronto squeezed an aptly named defenceman, Ken

Block, from L.A. as a concession. But the latter never played for the Leafs, made just one appearance later on for the Vancouver Canucks, and spent the majority of his time in the WHA.

McDonald soon found out his job description covered a lot more than calling goals and assists. Additionally, he had to prove to U.S. immigration that he could do this particular broadcasting job better than an American. McDonald had already beaten out a number of candidates, including fellow Canadian Dan Kelly.

The wily Cooke gave McDonald the title of assistant general manager to ease his employment status question with the U.S. authorities but then recruited him to run club media relations and what today is called director of team services. McDonald had to get the players to camp in Guelph, Ontario, and then find the best meal deal and accommodations. A well-known tightwad, Cooke restricted McDonald to spend no more than $9 per man per day. That was composed of $5 for hotels and $4 for food for a roster of about 70 players. Even with the lower prices 50 years ago, that was a challenge for anyone. "I managed to get the $5 hotel," McDonald said. "Then I pounded the pavement all over Guelph for restaurants—Chinese, Greek, whatever—trying to get a deal. I found a place that would serve breakfast for 75 cents and lunch for $1.25, leaving only $2 for the evening meal."

McDonald eventually found a golf course clubhouse in nearby Kitchener willing to do supper on the cheap at $2.25. "So I'm just 25 cents over budget. But Cooke comes back from England, where he was arranging the financing of the L.A. Forum, and says, 'Mr. McDonald, obviously you have no concept of math. Multiply that quarter by 70 players, and that's an astronomical amount.'"

The Kings chose Toronto's Terry Sawchuk with their first pick in the expansion draft's goaltender pool barely five weeks after he'd been in net for the Leafs' Cup-clinching game. But it was clear at the Kings' camp that Sawchuk didn't strike it rich in bonuses despite that championship. Much to McDonald's chagrin, Sawchuk decided to make some extra change ferrying players to the club's different breakfast and dinner locales in his car. But upset at losing the meal business, the Guelph hotel removed all TVs from the players' rooms in retaliation. "So you had no choice but to rent a set or watch the trains come and go from town," McDonald said.

* * *

Rick Wamsley's career as a colour commentator was brief. With the goaltending tandem of Grant Fuhr and Felix Potvin getting the lion's share of work early in the 1992–93 season, the quotable Wamsley was invited to fill in the radio booth for a road game in Los Angeles. But when Fuhr was pulled during a 6–4 loss, Wamsley had to rush downstairs and dress as Potvin's backup.

Assistant general manager Bill Watters replaced Wamsley for the balance of that game, returning to the gig he'd enjoyed before Fletcher hired him. Bowen teased him about why he was suddenly so lacking in criticism of the Leafs. Stellick also had a short career in the commentator's chair. He was asked to sit in with Bowen on the road when there was a void of colour men. Stellick was very qualified but could not resist a jab or two at some mistakes he saw on the ice during a difficult Leafs season. Word of his criticism got back to the players via their wives and friends who were listening, and Stellick wound up in a dressing room shouting match with centre Dan Daoust. His radio arrangement soon ended.

Issues between broadcasters and players or coaches do happen. Andrew Raycroft held the Leafs record for 37 wins, going into the 2018–19 season. After a particularly strong game, host Paul Hendrick had Raycroft at the boards on a live national network feed, which was also piped from the scoreboard, and innocuously observed how far Raycroft had come after a difficult first year. "Thanks for bringing that up," snapped Raycroft and skated off the ice, leaving Hendrick holding the microphone with his jaw agape. "All I could do was say, 'Okay, back upstairs to Joe and Harry,'" Hendrick said. "The next day I got an apology from Steve McKichan, the goalie coach. I said, 'Thanks, but I'll discuss this with Andrew personally.' We patched things up after a while."

Pat Quinn could be difficult as well. The 2004 Conference Semifinals with the Philadelphia Flyers highlighted Coach Quinn's mistrust of the media. In Philadelphia the Leafs cordoned off entrances to their dressing room, driving building staff crazy as they tried to do their daily jobs. When he felt a TV cameraman was getting too close to him during a one-on-one discussion with winger Tie Domi, he demanded the lensman turn over his tape on the spot.

He challenged a reporter's accuracy when asked about a back injury to Joe Nieuwendyk—only to have Nieuwendyk confirm he was hurt just minutes later. Asked about Mats Sundin telling trainers he wanted to be put back in Game 4 after an injury, Quinn dismissed the validity of the source, which was a quote from one of his own players. We won't get into Quinn's draconian policy of keeping ailments a secret—he was the grandfather of "upper and lower body injuries"—or his tight media access policies that saw the Leafs get fined thousands of dollars by the league. But years later when Quinn was trying to name his own choice as successor through the court of public opinion instead of ownership's, he suddenly became much more helpful to the scribes, detailing injuries, and even fishing players out of the room for reporters.

Gone Streaking

In October of 1993 after getting within a victory of the Stanley Cup final the previous spring, the Leafs burst from the regular season gate and won 10 straight. It was an NHL record and has been matched just once since. As the team pulled into Montreal for their next game, assistant general manager Watters was asked to do a phone interview with a Toronto radio station to talk about the streak. He couldn't resist having fun at the two hosts' expense. "Well, Cliff sat our whole staff down at the start of the year," Watters began in a serious tone. "And he was quite clear: 'if we're going to be 82–0 this year, it's really important we win the first 10.'"

A few seconds of dead air followed as the hosts tried to comprehend if Watters was on the level. Finally, one of them ventured a nervous laugh, and Watters eventually cracked up, too.

Prior to the 1998–99 season, the Leafs played an exhibition at Madison Square Garden.

Nick Kypreos, who was trying to hold his place on the team under new coach Quinn, took on rising New York Rangers tough guy Ryan VandenBussche. The fight, which happened right in front of reporters when MSG had the league's last ice-level press box, ended with a thundering punch from VandenBussche that left Kypreos in a pool of blood. He never played again.

After overcoming post-concussion syndrome, the retired Kypreos found a second career behind the microphone with Rogers Sportsnet. But he couldn't stand to watch his awkward early appearances and was almost fired after his first season, so he went back to basics. A lot of his segments were taped, and he transitioned back to live TV by studying more experienced broadcasters. He said colleagues such as Rob Faulds told him it could take someone in the profession as long as seven years to find a true comfort zone.

Kypreos compensated by working his many contacts—current and former Leafs, NHL coaches, executives, and media colleagues—and using all of them as sounding boards. That made him a key part of Sportsnet's trade deadline and free-agency team in their war with TSN in ratings-rich Toronto and across Canada. "When I first started the deadline shows, you'd take a breaking trade to the news desk. However, five or seven minutes might pass for you to wait until it was on the Internet. That was [agonizing]. It seems like the Stone Age now. But there was no one else in the business doing it except the two networks [Sportsnet and TSN]. The [scoop] I'm probably most proud of is the trade of Phil Kessel from the Leafs to Pittsburgh. We had seven or eight minutes [lead], which is a lifetime. We were supposed to go off the air but stayed on another hour to talk about it. It's still fun to break stories and be part of it—even if it's not like it used to be."

The salary cap era, a much earlier trade deadline, and intense competition from other news outlets took some steam out of the big midseason trade day. Whether it's the middle of the night or they're halfway around the world, some NHLers now take to social media to break their own deals. With the hockey world waiting on his decision to join the Leafs, John Tavares sent out a picture of him as a kid asleep in Leafs bedding. "Everyone's got Twitter feed, instant platforms, and broad access," Kypreos said.

Kypreos saw the irony in working the 2016 trade deadline, which fell on February 29. Exactly 20 years before—also in a leap year—Kypreos and winger Wayne Presley went to the Leafs in exchange for Sergio Momesso and Bill Berg going to the Rangers. Momesso and Berg also wound up as hockey analysts; Momesso went to TSN Radio in Montreal, and Berg went to the NHL Network. "At least we made it a few less former goalies," Kypreos said, laughing. "They had the [analyst] market cornered for years."

* * *

During the 1999 playoffs when the Leafs were playing the Pittsburgh Penguins, Joe Bowen and Jim Ralph, a former minor league goaltender, got around to talking about Pittsburgh ace Tom Barrasso. Bowen played up Barrasso's rare accomplishment as a high school grad who won the Calder Trophy and became an NHL star. "I know my dad was very proud of me for doing the same thing," said Ralph, sounding as syrupy as possible.

He knew that would get a rise out of Bowen, who jumped all over his sidekick, barking that he'd never played a minute in the Show, never mind winning any awards. "No, Joe, I was talking about finishing high school," Ralph said.

Another memorable exchange between the two came one night in 2003 at the Bell Centre in Montreal. The occasion was the banner raising to mark Jean Beliveau's 50 years with the Canadiens organization prior to a game against the Leafs.

It also happened to be the 50th wedding anniversary of Beliveau and wife, Elise, who was asked to write that loving message on the banner before it went up. The touching ceremony concluded with a standing ovation, which grew louder as the banner went up higher. Bowen and Ralph, by this time, had been through a few marriages between them, which they both often joked about. "Well, Joe," Ralph said above all the applause, "that's one banner they'll never raise for us."

A new member of the Leafs' broadcast crew came aboard in the mid '90s. Everything was fine until his first charter flight with the club for a road game. He had not revealed he was something of a queasy flyer, but that became obvious on the way home from the one-sided defeat when he fainted in the aisle. "Wow," deadpanned one veteran player as the guy was revived and helped into his seat. "He takes losing hard."

CHAPTER 5
MAPLE LEAF GARDENS

The site of the Maple Leaf Gardens was reputedly near an exchange of gunfire back in the Rebellion of 1837, when armed reformers under William Lyon Mackenzie were confronted by colonial government militia. Homes and small shops eventually occupied the land owned by the T. Eaton department store at Church and Carlton Streets until it was put up for sale by Eaton's, as the Great Depression began to sink in during the early 1930s.

J.P. Bickell, Conn Smythe, and other investors, who ran the NHL St. Patricks, realized at the end of the 1929–30 season that they needed to move out of the cramped Mutual Street environs. Their thoughts moved toward the Carlton/Church lot because of its proximity to streetcar lines and busy Yonge Street. But Eaton's initially was cool to the notion of parting with its land for a hockey arena, believing sports fans were too boorish to be congregating so near the new upscale store it had just opened on Yonge. Though the Eaton's people meddled in the artist's renderings of what the Gardens would look like, the company eventually did the civic-minded thing and backed the project, eventually investing in it.

Smythe fretted over every detail of the Gardens right up to opening night. As customers lined up at the various box office booths to purchase tickets for the November 12, 1931 opener against the Chicago Blackhawks, a curious Smythe moved from the back of each line to another, eavesdropping on the fans to get their take on the new facility. By doing so, Smythe actually aroused the suspicions of a police officer, who pulled him out of the line for questioning before the team manager could explain Smythe's behaviour.

Plodding waist deep in circus animal waste was not in Wayne Gillespie's job description when he came to 60 Carlton Street as an electrician in the mid-1970s. But his third day of work coincided with the Garden Brothers Circus having its annual residence—and led to a memorable first meeting with Harold Ballard. "We had a melting pit at the north end for the Zamboni when it dumped its load of snow," Gillespie said, "with a sump pump that dropped the water level if needed. But that area was also where they kept the elephants during the circus. As you can guess, they pee and crap a lot, and the tigers weren't much better. The pump backed up, and I had to get in there with hip waders to un-clog it. As I'm doing this awful, dirty job, I see this big man coming toward me. He says, 'Hello, son, how you doing?' I said, 'Not now, I'm really not in a good mood.' I had stopped following hockey as closely after the Original Six expanded, so I didn't really know the people associated with the Leafs management."

The New Star

Thanks to Foster Hewitt's initial radio broadcasts, Charlie Conacher was the Gardens' first true box office attraction and Leafs star personality. Conacher, a hometown boy, came from a large sports-loving family that included brother Lionel, Canada's Athlete of the Half Century (1900–50). He reached the 20-goal mark twice before the Leafs moved to the Gardens, scored the Leafs' first goal in the new rink, and continued to dominate on "The Kid Line" alongside Joe Primeau and Busher Jackson.

While the first souvenir goal puck from that game remains in the possession of the estate of Chicago Blackhawk Harold (Mush) March and was dropped by Marsh on closing night at the Gardens in 1999, Conacher's historic disc rarely leaves the mantle of the home of his son, Peter.

Charlie and Lionel opened a downtown gas station in 1935, a ceremony that caused a two-hour traffic back-up of men and boys who didn't want gas as much as an autograph. Both brothers reportedly developed stiff-armed writers' cramp that day from signing so much.

Ballard was miffed at being brushed off by an underling—and a new employee at that.

"When you get your first paycheque, make sure to go to the office to the door with my name on it," Ballard boasted to Gillespie. "Because my name will be the one on your cheque."

"Figuring I'd be looking for another job in about 30 seconds anyway, I replied right back, 'Your name might be on it, but so will mine, and mine will be ahead of yours," Gillespie said.

Shortly after, Gillespie was ordered to report to building super-intendent Don "Shanty" McKenzie. "What on Earth did you say to Mr. Ballard?" McKenzie asked. "He wants you to come up and work at his cottage. I have had guys that have worked here for 30 years, and they have never been asked to go to the cottage. You did it in three days."

Ballard had respect for those who stood up to him, and instead of getting fired, Gillespie had actually hit the right note. Joining Ballard's work crew at his cottage was considered the gravy train among the Gardens staff, and not only did Gillespie get this huge break, he also would later be selected to take over for McKenzie when the latter retired as building manager. "Mr. Ballard treated me great over the years and would sometimes send my wife, Denise, flowers on her birthday," Gillespie said. "To me there was nothing wrong with him, though I was fortunate enough to see his better side. He used to tell me, when he was in the midst of all kinds of criticism, how much he enjoyed it. 'I'm getting more press than the Prime Minister,' he'd say."

Ballard's cottage was at Thunder Beach in Midland on the shores of Georgian Bay. It was a great place for Gillespie and other staffers to be working in the offseason, though during one job stint, Ballard was away, and his lady friend at the time was in charge. "She'd adopt-ed a family of baby skunks and asked us to build them a box for a home. So one of the Gardens' carpenters made one with a hinged roof and everything. Baby skunks haven't developed the ability to spray, so it was okay to handle them and get them used to their new home. But the skunks grew older, and much later, when Harold was back, he came across the box. Not knowing what it was, he lifted the lid, looks inside, got really scared, and slammed it shut. That frightened the skunks, and they started spraying everywhere. We all ran for the hills."

Yolanda MacMillan, Ballard's girlfriend, also gave a pair of geese a winter home at the Gardens. Gifted to Ballard by Steve Stavro, when the latter was a company director, their wings were clipped so they couldn't fly at the cottage, but she fretted about their survival in the winter hockey season and had them brought to the team offices. They waddled around wearing diapers for a week until Ballard evicted them.

Of course, Gillespie's duties often took him inside the Gardens dressing room through the oversized wooden door that had been there since 1931. Captains from Hap Day to Mats Sundin had come through the same portal, and that entry was familiar to many people through *Hockey Night in Canada*. "You walk through that door, you're stepping back in time and hockey history," Gillespie said.

He was very proud of his place in the Gardens hierarchy and often could be found inspecting the front lobby where starstruck visitors came to look at the famous black and white photos of players and game action, going back to the dawn of the Leafs era in 1927. These enlarged images were put in simple blue picture frames assembled in the Gardens' carpentry shop.

Often, Gillespie would be touched to see an entire family come by to see such artifacts, and if they were out-of-towners or first-time visitors, he'd treat them to an impromptu tour of the building if his schedule permitted. "I'd take them into the Leafs room before the players arrived, the *Hockey Night in Canada* studio, the boiler room filled with all the old machinery and ice-making equipment and then let them sit in the penalty box. We always kept a minimum of 44 frozen pucks for a game on hand, and I'd give them one. It was real warm and fuzzy stuff for a Leafs fan. We'd end the tour at centre ice, where they could stand on the big Leafs logo for a picture," he said.

On one occasion Gillespie noticed a boy about nine or 10 years old who seemed overwhelmed by the whole experience. After he and his parents had their Kodak moment at centre, Gillespie noticed a yellow puddle had spread itself over the blue Leafs logo. "The kid just got too excited and peed himself," Gillespie said, laughing. "So I had to go in the workroom and get the guys to scrape it off. They were somewhat mad, but we all took it as a personal compliment that the building had such an impact on the young fan."

Gillespie was the go-to guy with fans, who had all manner of off-beat Gardens questions, because of his working knowledge of the inner sanctum. So many of them were fascinated with the building, which had captured their imaginations through radio and TV. "I don't know how these people would get my number, but I'd get all the unusual calls," Gillespie said. "One little old lady called me and asked what I did with the red line at centre ice in the summertime when the ice was out? I said, 'We freeze it,' joking with her. But she asked if she could have a piece of it, and I said by all means but told her she'd need to actually keep it in her freezer. [At season's end] I got a piece from the work gang, about 12" x 12" and took it over in a cab to this lady's apartment. You want to help people when you can. During the start of the next season, my phone rings. It's the lady, and she's a little upset she doesn't have her red line any longer. She said she took it out of the freezer to show her friends and forgot to put it back. I promised her at the end of that season I'd get her another piece, just one of those odd things."

Gillespie said it was critical to maintain Gardens' ice temperature even for late summer exhibitions and spring playoffs of the multi-use facility because the TV lights heated the surface about one degree every seven minutes.

Gillespie also supervised the various public service messages that were dabbed onto the ice during the hockey season, such as Cancer Awareness Month, United Way, and other promotions near and dear to Ballard's heart. But in later years, Gillespie lamented that the traditional Merry Christmas decoration was discontinued because of political correctness concerns. "Maple Leaf Gardens was a hockey rink; it was not about politics," he said.

Gillespie's workers did fret about a fire hazard with the four live Christmas trees that Ballard insisted be placed on each corner of the old green score clock in the '70s and '80s.

"When the clock was lowered and then put back, those trees would be up there two or three weeks with no water and fully lit," Gillespie said. "Thankfully, the carpenters, who put them there, knew to place them a little further back from the edge so the needles wouldn't start shedding on the ice during a game."

But a few things trickled down to the ice from the rafters, which rose to 135 feet. Deflating helium balloons from previous events such as concerts sometimes came to rest in the middle of a Leafs game. In the 1990s young *Toronto Sun* photographer Dave Abel went to a crow's nest vantage point in a long-abandoned catwalk for an overhead picture of the action. An old carpet at his feet began disintegrating as Abel was shooting, causing a black snow shower to fall upon Toronto netminder Felix Potvin, who looked skyward and alerted security to someone creeping around the rafters. But realizing what he'd done, Abel was able to escape and keep the story quiet.

Gillespie's electricians were sometimes assigned to the upper reaches for shows such as the Ice Capades, so that they could operate dimmers for the house lights over the ice surface.

"It was a very boring job," Gillespie said, "except for the Sunday matinee of the Ice Capades. Not many people would come to that one, so the staff would have some fun. There was a comedy team from Switzerland, Frick and Frack, who'd skate out [with] one of them playing piano near centre ice. Part of their routine was hearing the sound of a 'quack, quack' and one of them firing a loud fake gun skyward. Our guys working dimmers would throw a rubber chicken from the roof that landed on the ice. The audience loved it. One time we filled the chicken with water, so it would have some body when it hit the ice. But no one figured that it would go so much quicker with the extra weight, and for some reason, the piano was much closer to centre ice that day. It exploded, and we thought we'd killed the performer playing piano."

Gillespie also remembers the Gardens' green room, a temporary VIP setup near the visitors' dressing room at the north end of the building with food, drinks, and creature comforts for when the stadium hosted rock concerts or non-traditional indoor arena sports. At one tennis event in the '80s, the promoter brought in a pinball machine. Jimmy Connors was due to arrive, and a big deal was made to assure everything was just right for the former No. 1 player in the world. But then someone noticed the rather revealing art work theme featured on the machine was Connors' wife, former 1977 Playmate of the Year Patti McGuire. A blanket was thrown over it, and Gardens workers hustled to carry it away just before Connors was coming in.

Dealing with scam artists looking for money, free Leafs seats, or souvenirs was another part of Gillespie's job. And he had no time for such people. One woman wanted him to refund her Leafs ticket costs because her husband's seat was too small, even though they admitted to attending a wrestling match in the same place a week prior. A man wanted his cleaning bill paid when a fellow patron spilled beer on his suit, arguing it was Gardens' beer so it was the Leafs' fault. No one got reimbursed from Gillespie's office. "I have a hundred of those stories."

On a sloppy winter weather night, one middle-aged woman knocked on his office door and wanted the Leafs to pay for a new pair of suede boots because hers were supposedly ruined by the slush people tracked in from the streets to the Gardens' hallway. "Really?" He asked her. "And did you hover above the slush on the sidewalks to here without touching the ground?"

A Leafs game has yet to be canceled because of bad weather or internal maintenance problems, going back to opening night at the Gardens on November 12, 1931. But there were close calls with Mother Nature. In the 1960s the clean-up from rodeo horses wasn't completed before the ice was re-installed. Ugly brown patches started popping up, causing a delay.

Gillespie also recalled a game in the '80s that was imperiled—believe it or not—because there were no nets. "We used to store three sets of nets at the Gardens: for practice, for Marlie games, and the pro NHL nets," he said. "They were kept in the old bowling alley. We would pull the pro nets down for games on Wednesday and Saturdays at that time."

But prior to one match, workers found the mesh on both nets had been cut out—likely by a souvenir hunter. "Fortunately, our chief engineer Doug Moore—the inventor of de-ionized jet ice—had spare mesh in the boiler room in his office. One of the rink crew, a very patient guy, spent all afternoon stitching it back in," Gillespie said. "We could've used crappy nets or one with all the red paint on the posts and crossbars chipped off, but that wasn't how we did things at Maple Leaf Gardens. That would have been totally embarrassing. All of our nets were painted the brightest red, and when we had to replace rink board ads, we used hand sanders to remove puck marks and keep everything as white as possible."

Gillespie never thought he was totally alone in the Gardens. One of only three full-time building superintendents between 1931–99, he was often the last employee to leave at as late as 2:00 or 3:00 AM. Long after 16,000 people had departed, trainers had washed the sweaters for another day, the huge air fans were turned off, the floors were mopped, and the last bit of trash was placed outside, Gillespie would just sit in an empty gold or red seat and close his eyes. "You could still hear the crowd—regardless if it had been a hockey game or a rock concert," Gillespie said. "There might be just a couple of high overhead lights on, but the people were there. I would also think to myself, *Wow, now I get to be in charge of all this.*"

During their rounds overnight security guards would report mysterious sounds, which were chalked up to the wind or creaky doors, though perhaps not always. Gillespie recalled one evening in particular, when some famous Gardens residents apparently came back. "I always liked to walk down the halls of the east corridor where there were a lot of the old pictures, the same side as the dressing room: Red Kelly's first shift in Toronto as a Leaf, Ron Ellis holding his first goal puck," he said. "There was also one of The Kid Line. I'm alone, looking at that Kid Line picture, and, as I pass by, suddenly I sense the presence of all three of them in front of me, walking ahead and talking about some player on another team and how they were going to cover him the next game. It was like I was inside a James Lumbers illustration [the Canadian artist who specialized in historical photos melded with modern-day images of people and places]. I swear, I had to stop in my tracks, almost frozen until I came out of this trance. Whenever I'm asked how would I sum up my career at MLG, I answer, 'Very honoured and very proud.' Most of the public are on the outside looking in. Only a few of us were on the inside looking out."

Three Blind Mice

It's not easy to upstage Wayne Gretzky at the Gardens, but some rodents did in March of 1980.

During the game Borje Salming closed his hand on the puck in his own crease, and referee Ron Hoggarth signalled a penalty shot for Edmonton's Stan Weir. As Toronto players gathered to protest the call before Weir could shoot, a disgruntled fan somehow was able let some mice loose on the ice. They began scurrying about, while Weir kept circling, awaiting to be cleared to shoot. Maintenance men eventually corralled the rodents with huge scooper shovels, and Weir went on to beat Mike Palmateer as part of an 8–5 Oilers win.

Many older fans yearn for the days that they could lean right over the low-corner glass at the Gardens to watch warm-ups or see someone get up in the golds behind the unobstructed Leafs bench. But as NHL snipers developed curved blades and then went to light one-piece technology, it became clear why higher glass was installed all around the Gardens and why the protective netting was installed at Scotiabank Arena. The harder players could shoot, the higher the injury rate of fans and even team staffers were in the line of fire.

Graig Abel, the Leafs' photographer for 40 years until 2017, saw his share of carnage.

"This couple I knew, they sat three or four rows behind the Leafs bench," Graig Abel said. "The wife was a flight attendant and she got a puck right in the head one night and had to miss six months of work.

Worst part of that was that Ballard billed them for the ambulance ride that night. Her husband was mad enough to sue, but there are disclaimers on the back of the tickets about the risks you take at a game."

In another game the wife of a prominent doctor was also struck in the jaw by a puck, and the final bill was about $5,000 in dental work. Going back to the 1950s, ex-Leafs player Brian Conacher remembered coming to the Gardens for a front-row view with his mother to see his Uncle Charlie as coach of the Blackhawks. Charlie's status as a Leafs legend and Brian's father's Lionel being a local celeb assured the family great rink-side seats, though it had no protective glass or screen. Despite his mother warning him to be alert for wayward sticks and pucks, it was she who was clipped by Rocket Richard's lumber one night when the Montreal star came in too close to the boards.

A visit by the young gun Edmonton Oilers became Graig Abel's turn to visit the Gardens clinic. It was one of the first games Wayne Gretzky played in Toronto, so many of the local lensmen made sure to come out for the warm-up. Sans helmet and his locks flowing, No. 99 made for an ideal image. Hoping to get a picture that might be turned into freelance money for a hockey card or related promotion, Graig was also present. While snapping away, Abel didn't notice a few Oilers on the other side of the ice, testing the Gardens' glass while whipping high wraparound passes. While he looked down to check his camera settings, a puck cleared the rim and nailed him right between the eyes. "There was so much blood gushing I couldn't see," Graig said.

Wearing his white shirt that became stained bright red, he was quite the spectacle. Colleagues guided him to the tiny Gardens clinic near the dressing room for stitches and to get cleaned up while Graig could hear the kid who'd picked up the puck that struck him crowing about his souvenir. And who should be in the clinic, chatting with the trainers? "How in the hell did you get hurt?" Ballard asked. "The game ain't started yet."

Not wanting to tell the boss he was in effect working for the opposition, Graig told Ballard he was struck by accident while walking around the lower bowl. Graig declined Ballard's offer to have a team aide drive him to the hospital for further assessment and went back to his post in the end golds while wearing a giant bandage around one eye and still feeling dizzy. At one point he jerked the camera backward trying to follow the play, hit himself where the wound was fresh, and nearly passed out in pain.

Years later, Graig's son, Dave, was injured while positioned at the photographer's knot hole. A small pane in the corner that flips open to allow pictures unimpeded by scratches on the plexiglass or light reflections, it often doubles as a favourite post-practice pastime for players to try and shoot pucks through when no one's around. It wasn't a puck that got through to injure Dave, but the butt end of P.A. Parenteau's stick poked through in the heat of play and gave him a nasty concussion.

Steve Russell of the *Toronto Star* was nailed with a puck through the same opening. Toronto defenceman Luke Schenn dumped it in, and Buffalo Sabres goalie Ryan Miller unintentionally found the mouse hole with his hard clearing attempt. At least Russell gained something for his head injury. A contrite Miller saw what he'd done and after the game and gave Russell his goal stick.

*　　*　　*

In the Gardens era, Leafs doctors became just as familiar as the players positioned at the end of the bench in the gold rails. With its handle in easy reach of his seat, Leith Douglas relished the job of opening and closing the bench door on line changes. The media joked that the office door at his downtown private practice must have had a similar lever instead of a regular knob. During the '70s, '80s, and '90s a medical team that included Douglas, Michael Clarfield, Darrell Ogilvie-Harris, and dentist Ernie Lewis were on call for both clubs or if anyone in the crowd happened to be injured by a puck, shattered glass, or other mishap.

In what Ogilvie-Harris called one of the unit's shining moments in the late '90s, Leafs defenceman Mathieu Schneider took a high stick in the face early in the second period of a game. By the start of the third, the doctors had stitched up a lacerated eyelid, transported him a few blocks away to Wellesley Hospital to be checked for any sight damage, and got him back to the Gardens, where he scored the winning goal.

A few years earlier in 1993, little Siberian winger Nikolai Borschevsky was brought into the clinic with a sharp pain in his abdomen. Ogilvie-Harris detected a ruptured spleen and began making preparations for the player to undergo emergency surgery at a nearby hospital. He thought of getting help from a general surgeon familiar with the procedure, Dr. Ray Matthews, whom Ogilvie-Harris figured would be out having dinner at that time. He called anyway.

"When he answered, it was strange because I could hear the same noise in the receiver as I heard in my other ear. I said, 'Where are you, Ray?' And he replied, 'In the reds at the Leaf game.'"

Matthews quickly joined the Leafs staff, who got Borschevsky in an ambulance, and his spleen was removed later that evening.

* * *

Doug Gilmour thrived in the Toronto spotlight and in his role as captain. But his celebrity and his spontaneous acts of generosity did cause some grief in the team office in the Gardens era.

"Dougie had a heart of gold, which created a problem because the team had gotten so good so fast in the early '90s," Bob Stellick said. "Getting autographs was huge, of course. So all these kids were skipping school because there was money to be made hanging around the Gardens. Doug and Glenn Anderson came to me and asked to start a policy of no autographs on practice days so they could leave the building and not get mobbed in the street. Then one day our office was broken into. Somebody obviously wanted to get at our souvenir cupboard, and they took all our autographed sweaters, pictures, and stuff. They didn't even touch our expensive office computers. They wanted the Leafs' collectibles. We were going to call the cops, but Gilmour heard about the break-in. He told me, 'Don't do anything. I can get to the bottom of this.' He went straight to the kids in the street and said, 'Look, I know one of you did it. You'll never get another thing from me, so I want that stuff back.' Next day, Dougie showed up with three quarters of the missing merchandise."

For a while Gilmour lived in a small apartment in the hotel adjoining the Gardens, which was in proximity to a lot of needy people. "We had a call from a media outlet one day, asking to confirm that Doug was out there, giving away coats and sleeping bags," Stellick said. "When I asked, again he said not to mention anything. That was one of the most honourable things I'd seen anyone do."

Gilmour and coach Pat Burns also took a shine to a 14-year-old boy, whose birth defect gave him a dwarf-like appearance. The Children's Make-A-Wish Foundation brought him down to meet the team, where he immediately bonded with the captain and the coach. "They got him in our room, Burnsie walks in and just starts chirping away at him," Stellick said. "The kid was so excited. He was unusual-looking, and people were always treating him cautiously, maybe telling him he'd be okay, but here's Burnsie really giving it to him like he's one of the players. The kid made it down a couple of times more. When he died, I got a call from his mom, asking me to let Doug know. I didn't know what Doug would do, but he went to the kid's funeral. How proud that family must have been to have the captain of the Maple Leafs come to the service."

Gilmour also had a good sense of humor. When the Leafs practised at the Gardens, reporters and TV cameramen were allowed to stand near the benches and thus pick up some good colour for their stories as players and coaches fired one-liners back and forth. The players could also hear the scribes' banter as Gilmour did one day while doing some light skating between blue lines. Our idle talk that day was about which scene in *The Wizard of Oz* was the most frightening when we were kids. As we reminisced about the Wicked Witch of the West, flying monkeys, and such, Gilmour's ears perked up. He glided by and said, "You guys know Tie Domi was in that movie, eh? He's the Munchkin on far right of the Lollipop Guild song. The one in blue and white."

Presented with a trophy for scoring his 1,000th career point in 1996, Doug Gilmour also was known for his generosity and sense of humor off of the ice.

Orr Reaction

Wonderous defenceman Bobby Orr appeared in his first NHL game at the Gardens in 1966. "He played great of course," his old coach Harry Sinden recalled of the 3–3 tie. "But Foster Hewitt said to me he might need time in the minors."

Orr's talent and the fallout of the infamous Pat Quinn hit in the '69 playoffs did not make him a local favourite. "Bobby became the reason there was a Toronto-Boston rivalry," Sinden said. "They booed Bobby from the start in the Gardens. But they knew how good he was. It was a sense of frustration."

CHAPTER 6
HAROLD BALLARD

The boisterous Harold Ballard proved a very atypical boss for a young group of female secretaries who somehow kept the Maple Leaf Gardens hockey office running during his dysfunctional reign. In 1974 newly hired Pat Surphlis was given the additional job of finding food for Ballard's pet piranha named Fang. It was a gag gift from son Bill the previous Christmas. There had been two, but Fang soon ate his companion. Fang swam alone in a big tank by Ballard's office, where King Clancy would often tease him by sticking his fingers in the water.

Surphlis had to go to a local pet store every few days and secure some goldfish, Fang's favourite meal. The female shop assistant assumed Surphlis must have loved the breed, and that's why she was buying so many, so she took great care to find her the most colourful and healthy. Until Surphlis was in a hurry one day and asked her just to net the nearest goldfish as they wouldn't be around much longer. When the alarmed clerk heard what their fate would be, she began crying and threatened to call the police. Surphlis fled the store and found Fang another source for snacks.

A few years later, Surphlis found herself back at the Gardens as the media relations person for the Toronto Blizzard indoor soccer team, to which Ballard rented space. Bringing seasoned pros from around the world and plunking them in a hockey rink with the glass still in place was too much culture shock for many proud footballers. While some arenas put some effort into making their playing surfaces compatible, the Gardens was notorious for seams in the faux green turf that came apart during games. "I can still hear a couple of Scottish players getting their first look around and going "Aucchhh, naye," Surphlis said laughing. "At first some guys would fire the ball off the boards and wouldn't be ready when it came back and hit them in the head.

"If a shot was stopped and went high, the goalie would stand up and relax because he was used to it going into the crowd. But indoors the ball could come down, hit him in the head, and go in."

The entrepreneurial spirit lived in the Gardens in the Ballard era, as everyone seemed to turn a blind eye to private profiteering. "Before they sold beer in the building, ushers in the red seats would sell you liquor shots," Bob Stellick said, laughing. "If you bought a Coke and gave the guy an extra dollar, they had a shot to supply you with under their jackets."

The dodgy sale of standing-room-only spots also came under scrutiny. There was only supposed to be space for about 200 in that section before Stellick and ticket officials started nosing around after the game started. "There had to be at least 500 people up there, so many that you couldn't move," Stellick said. "Then we heard [employees] were letting people in for $5 through the back at the Wood Street entrance. We put a street camera there to find out what was going on, but just to show you how messed up things were: on the very first night, you see an usher walk up to the camera, take his jacket off, and throw it over the lens with his face still visible. He'd probably been making $100 a night for 20 years and now he's mad at us. Only in Toronto."

When the Soviet Union brought down a Korean Airlines passenger plane over its air space in 1983, it was around the time Ballard had finally relented to allow Russian teams to play exhibitions at the Gardens. The night that a Russian national side played the Canadian Olympic team, Ballard put up a message on the scoreboard: "Remember Korean Airlines Flight 007. Don't Cheer, Just Boo."

The Soviets were outraged, and one called Ballard "a hooligan." "We felt bad for doing that, so when one of their doctors knocked on our clinic door to ask for a couple of bandages, we let him in," Stellick recalled. "Next thing you know there are a couple of their guys in there, grabbing everything they can carry out of our supply cabinets."

The modern Leafs have tried to keep Ballard and his antics out of official club history—other than small bits such as acknowledging his election to the Hall of Fame as a builder.

They do devote an annual media guide note to one of his most ingenious stunts, which came during the 1977–78 season. When then-NHL president John Ziegler's decreed that all teams must put names on the backs of sweaters, Ballard was not about to take orders from someone he considered "a shrimp…insignificant…a paid employee."

Claiming Ziegler's rule would hinder program sales at the Gardens, Ballard refused to affix player identity. They were the only team to do so, though most everyone knew the Leafs' names and numbers through TV. Eventually, Ziegler thought he'd hit Ballard where it hurt—in the wallet—threatening a $10,000 fine for every game jerseys did not have names. He imposed a deadline of February 26, a game in Chicago, for Ballard to comply. Ballard got around that by putting blue letters on a blue nameplate on Toronto's blue road jerseys, making the surnames impossible to see. The Leafs won the game 5–3, and Ballard's act received lots of coverage. He also got away with it in their next road game on Long Island, but with Ziegler set to raise the fine, Ballard gave in. The players thought the controversy was a hoot, though centre Jimmy Jones added: "We were more concerned about Pops, the program seller at the Gardens for a very long time at the front entrance [and what would become of him]."

While Ballard could exhibit boorish behaviour to many, including his own family, he was overly generous with Christmas gifts. The Leafs' holiday swag became the envy of the NHL, sometimes including two airline tickets anywhere in North America or the world. But if you were a fringe player in the '80s and the league's December roster freeze was imminent, a bubble boy would sometimes find himself on the farm during Christmas and thus miss out on the loot.

After Ballard's passing—and with salaries taking an upward turn—the club backed away from exorbitant gifts and started making donations to charity causes.

In another devious move in the late '80s, Ballard found a way to deny both the progressive movement to let female media in the dressing room and piss off the entire Toronto press corps. More American newspapers were hiring women to cover the NHL, and teams changed with the times to permit access—except Ballard's Leafs. "They can go in the room, but they have to take their clothes off, too," he teased.

But when the Toronto chapter of the Professional Hockey Writers Association (PHWA) demanded equal access, Ballard seized on the term "equal" and used the language to keep all reporters out. It was quite troubling for all media, but newspapers on deadline—long before the Internet—suffered most. Ballard was already at war with *The Globe and Mail*, banning some of its highly critical columnists from the premises and was quite pleased with this latest skullduggery. The league felt its hands were tied on the matter and didn't act in support of the scribes.

Ken Daniels of CBLT-TV chased down Ballard at the door of the Leafs room at the Gardens. With his cameraman rolling, he asked the owner to explain his objection to women being allowed to do their jobs. "I can't let them in," Ballard barked. "Some of those players have cocks as long as my arm."

"Harold, you can't say that on air," said a shocked Daniels, motioning his guy to stop filming.

"Why not?" Ballard protested. "It's true."

The situation wasn't resolved for months and it only stoked the anger of reporters in Toronto and elsewhere who were forced to wait longer to interview Leafs. In November of 1987, Scott Morrison of the *Toronto Sun* and then-PHWA chapter chairman, decided it was time for a "Charge of The Write Brigade." Each of the big papers sent a full complement to cover the match. After waiting the league-mandated 10 minutes following the game, Morrison pushed open the dressing room doors and led the way through. Galvanized by the writers' action, the large radio and television presence came in a second wave, all fanning out to interview players. "Is this Christmas?" asked one confused Leafs player.

The media didn't linger long after making its point. That was a good thing because despite being confined to a wheelchair at the time, Ballard got word of the revolt and had his assistant roll him at high speed through the halls to the scene, where he got in a swing at a *Globe* photographer with his cane. "Guerilla warfare broke out last night at the Gardens," chirped Mike Rutsey of The Canadian Press in his report of the incident.

Beefy general manager Gerry McNamara, who was also at odds with the media at the time, was not around that evening. He later called his absence one of his greatest regrets on the job, having missed out on a possible physical confrontation with some of his harshest critics. But Ballard was beaten on the issue, and the walls came down.

By the summer of 1989, the front-office structure of the Leafs could not have been more fractured. An increasingly unstable Ballard had sidelined youthful GM Gord Stellick in favour of coach George Armstrong, who didn't want the job and only wished to return to scouting. Armstrong had already delegated the day-to-day on-ice responsibilities to assistant coach Gary Lariviere—much to the chagrin of Stellick.

As Stellick tried to do his own job, maneuvering around the muddled situation, Ballard was constantly playing up Armstrong as the team's next saviour. He told Stellick that Armstrong was "the greatest thing since 7UP" and advised one reporter that Armstrong should be considered "the head potato" on the team, all the while ordering Stellick not to speak to the media as it would keep himself out of the headlines.

Ecstatic to be selected by the Leafs on draft day, junior players often had a memorable introduction to Ballard. At the 1988 event in Montreal, Ballard spotted the mullet on first rounder Scott Pearson and right away snapped, "Get a haircut," though Pearson was out of earshot. Ballard had uttered the same thing during a face-to-face meeting with second rounder Daniel Marois the year before in Detroit, but Marois did not understand English at the time.

Paying Clark

With a beaming Wendel Clark still lingering at the Leafs draft table with Bob Stellick after going first overall in 1985, Ballard remembered he hadn't worked out a salary for Stellick to run the media and public relations department. "How much ya want?" Stellick recalled of Ballard asking him right in front of the 18-year-old Clark. "I told him I made $28,500 at Central Scouting—really $23,000—but I'd lied. So he grumbled and said 'I'll give ya $27,000.' When I asked about benefits, he said, 'Whatever your brother has.' [Gord was the de facto assistant GM at the time.] It turned out Gord made just $20,000. So the next day, Harold had to give Gord a raise to $30,000. And I'm sure Wendel is sitting there thinking, *Is this the NHL or the Saskatoon Blades?*"

One of the biggest miscalculations Ballard made was the impact of the World Hockey Association in the early '70s. It was big money that the old-guard NHL was initially reluctant to dole out to keep its stars. Once the new outfit was up and running, more players started defecting. "Harold didn't have people around to counsel him on what to do about the WHA," Bob Stellick said. "So he went to someone he knew very well, the league president Clarence Campbell. He was a respected lawyer, who had worked all the way back in the Nuremberg trials during World War II. But Clarence was over the hill by then. He assured Harold the WHA would not last more than four months and told him not to pay any of his players, who were threatening to go there. So Harold said to his best Leafs, 'Screw you.' It meant we lost about nine or 10 players [including Keon, Paul Henderson, Norm Ullman, and nearly Darryl Sittler]. We were decimated by the WHA."

Ballard's spite kept up during the decade, and he also voted to block the first attempts at a WHA-NHL merger to bring in more Canadian teams. Part of the reason Ballard was so frugal about sharing TV money was that his lines of credit were stretched thin to maintain control of the Gardens. "He bought everything on debt through the Toronto Dominion Bank and Molsons Brewery," Stellick said. "If he'd been a richer guy or had a son who could be his advisor, it would've been different. That's the tragedy—that no one was able to take over for him. He went out and did things like buy the Hamilton Tiger-Cats [of the Canadian Football League] when they were losing about $4 million a season. We could've bought Gretzky every year for that kind of money. But Harold probably saved the CFL because of what he did, and that's why he's in their Hall of Fame, too."

Stellick could spin a million stories about Ballard but never failed to mention his gratitude to the owner who gave him his start in the hockey business world and the successful marketing firm that he runs today. And if some account in Ballard's long list of perceived misdeeds is false or exaggerated, it's Stellick who will set the record straight. "People look back and say Harold treated the alumni terribly. Well, he made Johnny

Bower a scout and hired Dick Duff when some teams would not have given those older guys the chance," Stellick said. "Our head carpenter's wife got cancer, and Harold quietly paid to send her to the Mayo Clinic. Harold tried to go to the funeral of anyone who worked at the Gardens—even the lowliest usher. My brother joked that we were first class in all the wrong things. Gord Finn, our head box office manager, used to say Harold had been such a fun guy before he unexpectedly ended up owning an NHL team. The only person he could think of to emulate was Conn Smythe, and Conn had been very hard on people. Harold thought that was how you had to do it. His behaviour was up and down, but he owned the team. If you Google the Harold Ballard Foundation, it still exists. There is a new rehab hospital in Toronto called Bridgepoint with a garden that has his name, and the Salvation Army has the trucks that have the Foundation's name."

CHAPTER 7
THE SUPER '70S

Actor Art Hindle was able to embed himself in this particular period of loose Leafs history. Cast as bad boy Billy Duke in the Canadian-made movie *Face-Off* in 1971, he was permitted to practice and even travel with the team to immerse himself in the role of a talented, but troubled, star. The Halifax native joined hellraisers such as Jim McKenny and Jim Dorey (both Leafs defencemen were wannabe actors once considered for the movie's title role) on a road trip late in the 1970–71 season. After a 1–1 tie in Philly, many Leafs were at a local watering hole when Hindle checked his watch and noted it was nearing 1:00 AM, coach John McLellan's curfew. Laughing teammates advised him not to worry. "John has to tell us that," McKenny explained as the party continued at ex-Leafs goalie Doug Favell's house.

When the trip moved to California, members of the California Golden Seals stopped by Leafs practice and saw Hindle struggling to keep up. Not knowing who he was, they mocked his skills until Paul Henderson warned them Hindle was a minor league goon who might flip at any moment if put into the game. The trip helped Hindle's character development to the point he slept in and missed a flight and had to catch up to the Leafs at his own expense. McLellan did not spare him from a team fine. "We knew he was a real player after that," McKenny laughed.

In searching for American distribution before completing *Face-Off*, Canadian producer John Bassett (his father owned the *Toronto Evening Telegram*, TV station CFTO, and was once a part owner of the Leafs) faced a major hurdle. "That kind of deal was very important for success in those days and still is now," Hindle said. "Cannon Distributing out of Boston loved our film (the U.S. version would be titled *Winter Comes Early*) except they told John they wanted more 'heat' in it."

Reluctantly, Bassett and director George McCowan came up with a bedroom sequence where Hindle and co-star Trudy Young were to shed their equipment, so to speak. "We went up to CFTO and on a sound stage. They put a bed and some curtains," Hindle said. "That was all. It looked just like a porno set. Remember, Trudy had been on kids' shows [CBC's *Razzle Dazzle* in her teens]. She was Canada's sweetheart. They said to her, 'Wear this nice little negligee.' Trudy and John hated the whole idea, and I was nervous, too, but Trudy changed and got into bed with all these cameras pointed at her. Now they're waiting for me to come from my dressing room into bed with John shouting, 'Hurry up!' So as a joke, I come bouncing out in full hockey regalia with skates and holding my stick, jump on the bed, and yell 'Okay baby, let's go!' Everyone was laughing—Trudy, the crew, and John. Eventually, John said, 'That's it. We aren't shooting this.'"

* * *

In Toronto music annals, the joke used to circulate about how many people actually saw The Police in their first appearance at The Horseshoe Tavern in the late '70s. The estimate was about 30, but over time it somehow multiplied to about 30,000 who insisted they'd been there.

It was much the same with those claiming to have witnessed Darryl Sittler's 10-point game firsthand on February 7, 1976. Maple Leaf Gardens held less than 17,000 at the time, but many more insisted decades later they were present to see him make history.

One account we certainly do trust was future voice of the Leafs and Foster Hewitt Award winner Joe Bowen, who was then working at CKSO radio in Sudbury, calling games for the junior Wolves. As a reward for covering some downhill skiing events up north for station sponsor Inco mining, Bowen and five colleagues were given Leafs tickets to that fateful Boston Bruins encounter. As young men from the north in the big city for the weekend, things were well into party mode by Saturday night, and Bowen's group was noticeably overserved by the time they wobbled into the Gardens. Sittler had six goals and four assists, a record that still sands. "I always tell Darryl, 'I heard you had quite a game because I sure don't remember much of it,'" Bowen said, laughing.

One of Bowen's pals, having already thrown his hat on the ice after Sittler's first three goals, was looking for anything to toss after the record-breaking ninth point. He began trying to extricate the cushion

Sporting the Maple Leafs' new jersey in 2011, Darryl Sittler is well-known for his 10-point game in 1976, a contest many fans claim to have attended.

from his gold seat. "He actually did it," Bowen said, "but before he could haul it up and over the glass, the ushers kicked him out and he missed Sittler's 10th point."

In this age of sports collectible mania, where entrepreneurs theme their restaurants, build personal museums, and travel the world in search of the arcane of athletics, it's always fascinating to recall how little memorabilia used to matter. Case in point was the DNA of Sittler's 10-point game against Boston's unfortunate goaltender Dave Reece. It might still be the record for a few decades to come—given the vast improvement in goaltenders and their gear.

Yet Sittler didn't retrieve a single puck from that night, while his stick ended up in the hands of team trainer Joe Sgro and was apparently lost in a garage fire. Most surprising of all, his sweater went missing, too. Sittler could never find out where the white No. 27 with blue trim ended up and just assumed it was lost. In those days clubs only issued two or three home and road jerseys that were expected to be kept in good shape by the player or maintained by equipment staff. "Today you might wear a third jersey just in warm-up and never put it on again," Sittler said.

But in 2018 on the 42nd anniversary of his great game, Sittler was informed his sweater had been recovered—albeit locked away in a New Jersey warehouse. TSN's Frank Seravalli aired a story on collector Barry Meisel, who had bought it from an unidentified dealer. It had previously passed between four or five owners, who'd all kept quiet about its existence. "We played the next night after the 10 points," recalled Sittler, who was held to an assist against the Minnesota North Stars, "but I really had no idea if I had the same sweater on or if it was already taken."

The TSN story claimed Ballard had procured it as a gift to a friend, which Sittler says is plausible. However, no collectors approached him in the ensuing decades. Meisel, who keeps an estimated 10,000 game-worn jerseys in the warehouse, received a call one day in 2017 about purchasing nearly 90 vintage sweaters. When he heard one was Sittler's, he gave it special attention. "We knew it was a '75–76, knew it was game worn," Meisel said. "Needles in the hay stack are fine, but when you see the needle's made of gold, and all you have to do is dive into the stack, it makes it very exciting."

He made a special trip to the Hockey Hall of Fame's resource centre in suburban Toronto to see what might exist in terms of photographs and other images of the 10-point outing. Meisel and the Hall of Fame staff carefully examined each one, detecting the stem on the Ballard era Leafs crest Sittler wore was a bit crooked, and a white thread was clearly dangling from one of the shoulder numbers. "And there was one beautiful picture perfectly positioned of his arm, where the blue stripe had that unique white blemish," Meisel said. "Same shape, same place, same size. That gave us three points of absolute uniqueness. We knew we'd found it."

How much would it be worth as the 50th anniversary of Sittler's feat approaches within the next decade? Based on the $1.27 million U.S. paid a few years ago for Paul Henderson's Game 8 Team Canada sweater from the Summit Series, the 2018 estimate was that Sittler's will fetch between $350,000 to half a million.

Meisel says he might hold off selling his treasure to the highest bidder, hoping it can be purchased by a person or institution, which would make sure the sweater goes on public display. Sittler, who does not seem keen on bidding himself, shares that sentiment. "He authenticated it, and if he wants to [keep it public], that's great. I had followed the Henderson sweater story. If [Meisel] gets enough money for it, he has the right to do what he wants, and I respect his right. Who'd have thought they'd find it after all this time anyway?"

Coincidentally, friends in the Canadian sports TV industry had given Sittler a custom VHS of his 10-point highlights. It was never reproduced, so he would have the most special of keepsakes. But he regretted losing it during a change of houses many years ago, figuring it might have been loaned out or forgotten in a tape machine that he'd thrown out.

* * *

In Christmas of 1972, scout Gerry McNamara was to fly to Sweden to watch goalie Curt Larsson at an international tournament. The door to Europe was opening up a crack after the Canada-Russia series a few months earlier, and McNamara wanted to find out what he could on Larsson and his club team in Sodertalje. He was also to report on any other players of note.

Arriving in Stockholm, he happened to catch a tournament game between a visiting Canadian senior team, the Barrie Flyers, and Brynas, a local club. The game was notable for two Brynas players: defence-man Borje Salming and winger Inge Hammarstrom. Salming stood out, not just for his fluid play and skating, but also for standing up to a belligerent Barrie player and getting tossed when he accidentally hit a referee during the scrum. "I couldn't believe what I was watching," McNamara said. "I followed him to the room, knocked on the door, the trainer opened it. I handed Borje my card and said [very slowly for translation purposes] 'You...play...for...Toronto Maple Leafs?' He said, 'Yeah.' Then I said, 'Inge play for Leafs?' He said, 'Yah, see Inge. Better English.' I phoned home and said to get them on our negotiation list right away."

McNamara returned the following spring with Toronto's chief scout Bob Davidson to watch the world championships in Moscow. Salming was once more dominant, but McNamara also spied Swedish forwards Anders Hedberg and Ulf Nilsson. They didn't sign. McNamara suspected that Hedberg was turned off by Davidson's brusque manner, though he kicked himself years later for not adding them to his negotiation list.

Those two went on to star with the Winnipeg Jets of the WHA and later the New York Rangers. Hedberg, who later scouted for the Leafs, held a senior management position and is now on the selection committee for the Hockey Hall of Fame. But McNamara was very content to land Salming a future All-Star, Hall of Famer, and the current franchise assist leader with 620.

"Borje was from northern Sweden and tough as nails," McNamara said. "I'd go in our room after a game against the Philadelphia Flyers, and his body looked like a pin cushion from all the spears. But he never backed off an inch. He's one of the all-time best in the NHL, and I'd take him over anybody, except maybe Bobby Orr."

Harold Ballard had his Leafs favourites, who had many gifts lavished upon them. Salming was valued above all else, especially after the owner's early '80s fall-out with Sittler. Salming was one of the few Leafs who Ballard could still recognize as he reached his 80s and was the recipient of contract largesse from a frugal owner. Unfortunately, the more reserved Hammarstrom did not absorb NHL punishment as well as Salming, nor did he hit it off with the boss. When the winger's goal production fell after a few years, Ballard kept needling him in the newspapers. In a scathing quote many said was fed him by crony King Clancy, Ballard scoffed that Hammarstrom "could go into the corner with six eggs in his pocket and not break one."

It wasn't long after that at the start of 1977–78 that Hammarstrom was traded to St. Louis. Salming deeply regretted his club made the move. He insisted that had his good friend not played in the rock-'em, sock-'em era, his skills would have made him just as famous in Toronto as himself. Yet the Ballard-Hammarstrom story did not end there. Fast forward to the 1989 draft in Bloomington, Minnesota, when Hammarstrom worked for Central Scouting. Despite very poor health, the wheelchair-bound Ballard insisted on going and sitting at the Leafs table with all the staff. But the attendant pushing his chair that day took the ramp at draft floor level too fast, and Ballard was jerked forward, heading straight for the concrete floor—only to be caught by Hammarstrom, who happened to be standing at the gate.

A couple of years later working for Philadelphia, Hammarstrom received much of the credit for prodding the Flyers to draft future Hall of Famer Peter Forsberg. Hammarstrom also was associated with new skate sharpening technology that brought him back to the Gardens.

* * *

New netminders Dunc Wilson and Doug Favell caused a dress code sensation at Toronto's training camp in 1973, when they showed up to the first team meeting in shorts and T-shirts. "Jim Gregory spotted us and he was pretty angry," Wilson said. "He told us, 'This is the NHL, and you always wear a shirt, tie, and cut your hair.' We walked into the Gardens, and, sure enough, everyone had shirt and ties. Even McKenny had a Western lariat around his collar. But they took one look at us and said, 'Hey, if the goalies can dress like that, why can't we?' By the end of the season, we even had Dave Keon wearing jeans and Kodiak work boots."

But the late coach, Red Kelly, chose that season to experiment with an unconventional three-goalie rotation: Wilson, Favell, and veteran Ed Johnston. "You played, you backed up, and you sat," Wilson said. "The three of us got along, but the problem was that you lose a tenth of a second reaction time when you sit that long."

Wilson also became one of the first Leafs goalies with a painted design on his mask, two distinct stripes, an intersected "X" that might have been incentive for shooters to aim at his noggin and fire high over the net. He and mask artist Greg Harrison later decorated the bars and added red and blue when Wilson joined the Rangers. Unfortunately, it also resembled a crude Confederate flag. "They loved it in the South when we played Atlanta but not many other places," Wilson said. "I even had a death threat phoned in to the team."

Golf Course Hijinks

In the late 1970s—long before the Tampa Bay Lightning and Florida Panthers—the Leafs were afforded a few days off to golf in Florida. High spirits on the links got out of control one day, and a golf cart was tipped over, leading to some unflattering headlines back home. "It was Borje Salming, but [as the young guy] I got the blame for it," said future coach Randy Carlyle.

The fallout added to tension between Carlyle and coach Roger Neilson, not to mention the end of the annual Florida holiday for the rest of the Leafs.

CHAPTER 8
ROAD TRIPS

Pat Burns was the last Maple Leafs coach to work in Original Six arenas, such as the Maple Leaf Gardens, the Montreal Forum, and Chicago Stadium, but the most dilapidated in his opinion was Boston Garden. "After a Canadiens practice there one day, [assistant coach] Jacques Laperriere and I are getting dressed," Burns said. "He bent over to pick up what he thought was one of his grey socks—until the sock scurried away into a hole in the wall."

Burns would eventually work in Boston, but not until the TD Garden was built next door.

When playing in Boston in the Cliff Fletcher era, the Leafs often dined by the water at the Essex Seafood Restaurant run by Dr. Robert Offenberger, whose day job was team psychologist, the first the club had appointed. But Offenberger's establishment was twice flooded in his Leafs tenure, including a side swipe in 1991 from Hurricane Bob. A storm the next year caused even more damage. "In the 75 years before I bought it, it flooded only twice," a saddened Offenberger reported. "In the 10 years I've had it, it's happened four times. An employee called me and said, 'Hey boss, the catch of the day is at my feet.'"

*　*　*

On one trip to Los Angeles, the Leafs decided to stay at the haunted Biltmore Hotel in L.A. The staff relayed the ghost stories to the players and that its bar was still home to the spirit of the Black Dahlia, an aspiring actress brutally murdered in the 1940s and whose killer was never found. Other apparitions of soldiers and nurses from its time as a World War II convalescent facility persisted in legend—as did the mysterious giggling sounds of a child. "We also heard there was an elevator sealed shut since a worker fell to his death and that the first and second floors are completely empty because there are supposed to be ghosts roaming them," said Leaf Nation Network's Paul Hendrick.

Creative Leafs players decided it was a perfect opportunity to prey on the fears of Darcy Tucker. "Bryan McCabe, Darcy's roommate, was

Pat Burns, the last Maple Leafs coach to work in Original Six arenas, leads a practice session in 1994.

in on it first," Hendrick said, laughing. "He stalled Darcy in the lobby long enough to allow Tom Fitzgerald and Ed Belfour to sneak up into the room. Tom gets under the bed, Eddie in the closet. Enough patience was involved for them to wait a whole half hour until Fitzy started pulling on the end of the covers ever so slightly to startle Darcy, and then Eddy started scratching on the closet door. Darcy jumped up so high he nearly wound up in the other bed with Bryan, who was scared out of his wits. For someone who would dive into the bench in Ottawa to take on all their guys, he was petrified of ghost stories.

Pat Quinn just loved all the old hotels in the league, such as the Palliser in Calgary and the Chateau Laurier in Ottawa."

Those weren't the only moments of horseplay on the road. The old Bloomington Airport Marriott, next to the Met Center home of the North Stars, was often the site of trouble for the Leafs. Isolated in the dead of winter, bored players tried to make their own fun, including some Nerf games in the hallways. "Borje Salming and some guys got kicked out by management for acting up," Bob Stellick said. "Borje called me and asked if I could get his clothes out of the room because he and some others had to stay next door at this smaller hotel, the Thunderbird. But despite crazy things like that, Borje still loved being a Leaf."

Unusual Press Conference Location

The expansion Tampa Bay Lightning began playing out of Expo Hall on the state fairgrounds with its capacity of just a bit more than 10,000. The Leafs debuted there October 22, 1992, and two Rob Pearson goals paced a 5–2 win. It was close enough from the bench to the press box that coach Burns could make direct eye contact with general manager Cliff Fletcher, adding crumpled facial expressions if he was angry with some mistake one of the boss' favourite players had made.

But feeling too constricted in Expo's tiny hallway after the game, Burns brought the media out on the lawn to hold his presser under the stars. The unusual setting prompted beat writer Frank Orr to crack "Coach, I've never done one of these *al fresco* before."

When the Leafs came back to the Eastern Conference, beginning in the 1998–99 season, many purists rejoiced. It restored them on the same grid as the Montreal Canadiens, their ancient enemies from Quebec, and the Buffalo Sabres, their closest geographical rivals. The quick upturn in Leafs fortunes under their new coach, Quinn, that season meant an edge on the Habs, especially in goal, where Curtis Joseph proved difficult for Montreal. But the Leafs still could not enjoy success against Buffalo, going back to its 1970 arrival in the league. Former Toronto GM/coach Punch Imlach re-surfaced on the other side of the Peace Bridge and spanked the Leafs 7–2 in that first meeting.

For years after, no matter how many Leaf fans made the two-hour drive to pack Memorial Auditorium or First Niagara Center (the latest name change of the current rink), Toronto was usually on the losing end. It tried every change in routine it could think of from arriving at the last minute, coming in the day before, staging morning skates in Toronto, or having no morning skate at all. Buffalo still held an advantage of 64–30–6–6 at the start of the 2018–19 season.

In 1999 the Leafs did have an excellent chance to beat the Sabres on the big stage. It was the first playoff meeting between the clubs—in the Eastern Conference Final, no less. The Leafs even had an apparent gift-wrapped Game 1 at the Air Canada Centre when Buffalo's enigmatic goaltender, Dominik Hasek, took himself out before the match with a mysterious injury. But the Leafs couldn't get past backup Dwayne Roloson and lost 5–4. They did recover to win Game 2, but Hasek came back in the series, and Toronto dropped the next three. "Yeah, we had some wild games against them," said Buffalo enforcer Rob Ray. "Tie Domi and I had our differences, but that was hockey at the time. I will say: after what Dominik did to us, to win that series right in Toronto in Game 5…let's just say that was one very satisfying bus ride back to Buffalo. They thought they had us and they were going to the Stanley Cup final."

Weather has played a big role in delaying the Leafs in various forms of travel, though officials and support staff make every conceivable attempt to get them to the game on time. Getting home can be tricky as they found out on December 26, 2010, in Newark, New Jersey, at the new Prudential Center. While many events in the area were canceled as highways became nightmares, Leafs-Devils was given the green light. An announced crowd of just 5,329 made it, mostly straggling into town via public transit.

Afterward, two buses carrying the Leafs and their broadcast team braved the blizzard for what should have been a 30-minute drive to the airport. It turned into a four-hour ordeal, as they inched past stalled and spun-out vehicles. Eventually, the media bus slipped off of the road, and the players had to come out of their shuttle and help radio and TV people push it back on the pavement. That irony had a further comedic touch when Hendrick would not help the rescue effort. He had been given an expensive pair of dress shoes for Christmas and feared ruining them in the slush. The team never made it to the snowbound airport. They found a highway exit and eventually checked into a small hotel. A second attempt to leave next morning was also thwarted. The Leafs made it to the airport this time, but the plane could not take off. They eventually departed that night.

CHAPTER 9
THE '80S AND '90S

Rick Vaive was excited for his first look at the Toronto franchise's 75th anniversary highlight video but was not pleased afterward. "The '80s got only two minutes of coverage," the former captain said ruefully of his era.

Yet Vaive should not have been too surprised. Although there have been some lean times in the ensuing decades—a then-club-record seven straight years out of the playoffs between 2006 and 2012—there was little comparison to the train wreck that came after the Darryl Sittler years in the late '70s and the arrival of Cliff Fletcher in 1991. In between was a Dark Ages of dashed hopes, ruined prospects, goofy headlines, and general degradation laid to rest beneath a tombstone of 441 losses, 260 wins, and 91 ties. "Disarray was everywhere from top to bottom," Vaive said. "No question we were something of a product of everything that went on around us. As players we have to take some of the blame, but when players can't develop and systems aren't conducive to the team, then you have problems. It just wasn't a well-run, well-oiled machine that developed great draft picks."

Teams that started from scratch—the New York Islanders and Edmonton Oilers—became dynasties in the '80s, while the Pittsburgh Penguins and Calgary Flames also won the Stanley Cup for the first time. The Leafs, by comparison, were dying a slow death played out on the national stage. Confronted by a reporter about why the Leafs didn't follow more of the Oilers' model after they'd won four titles in five years that decade, Harold Ballard harrumphed, "Edmonton? What have they ever done?"

"In my time with the Leafs [1983–91], I saw eight head coaches and four GMs," winger Gary Leeman said.

Not to mention that two captains, including Vaive, were defrocked, rough characters such as Paul Higgins and John Kordic became *cause celebres*, and almost every dressing room spat found its way into the headlines. Even marital woes became fodder for newspapers. Sittler was the first casualty at Christmas of 1979, snipping the "C" off his sweater in a fit of anger when general manager Punch Imlach tried to undermine his dressing room power base by trading good buddy Lanny McDonald to the Colorado Rockies. But more long-lasting damage would be done to a promising crop of youngsters.

Defencemen Jim Benning, Fred Boimistruck, and Bob McGill, chosen sixth, 26th, and 43rd overall, respectively, were all moved up together between 1981–83, and those two seasons yielded 84 losses and more than 700 goals against. "You just never saw that in pro sports," Vaive said. "You just knew we were asking for it."

At the time players, such as Boimistruck, were thrilled to jump from junior right into the pro ranks. But the sink-or-swim mentality of management would backfire without a developmental gameplan. "Like any other junior, I realized a dream of playing in the NHL in my first year," said Boimistruck, a two-time Memorial Cup champion with the Cornwall Royals. "But I found myself on a losing club, and my confidence level went down with it. I found the game changed for me, and the fun got sucked out of it. That I was given such an opportunity was unbelievable, yet there is some bitterness that goes with the way things turned out. It was like going to war when you had never been shot at."

Boimistruck did not stay too long in the game after the Leafs but later found some peace and contentment with his second love—trains. He became a Via Rail engineer on a Northern Ontario route.

During a New Year's Eve game against Detroit in 1981, injuries forced the call-up of two more kids, Craig Muni, who was also a high draft pick taken 25th overall in 1980, and Darwin McCutcheon. That put five underagers on the same blue line. Amazingly, the Leafs won that match. McGill, who went on to coach the Oshawa Generals and become a commentator for Leafs Nation Network, said the symptoms were not alleviated as the '80s unfolded. "It wasn't just [Benning, Boimistruck, and himself], but Al Iafrate and Luke Richardson [also first-round defencemen] had problems."

In the net it wasn't much better. It was a chicken-and-egg conundrum, where the weak defence made life hard on many green starters who badly needed support in front of them. "Just look at the goaltenders that were on the team while I was there," Vaive said, "Paul Harrison, Curt Ridley, Mike Palmateer, Rick St. Croix, Ken Wregget, Vincent Tremblay, Jiri Crha…we went into Winnipeg one night, where they were hardly a dynamo at the time and lost 10–1."

McNamara's selections should have done much better, at least on paper. The group also included first rounders Russ Courtnall, Iafrate, Clark, Vince Damphousse, and Richardson. Chosen not far behind were Leeman, Peter Ihnacak, and Todd Gill. All would have noteworthy careers but few as Leafs. "Take a look at my drafts and the ones since I left and tell me we didn't do well," McNamara responded. "Every one of my first rounders went to the NHL and never played a game in the minors other than Gary Nylund, who went down for [injury] rehab. My last draft [in 1987], six guys went to the NHL."

McNamara would regret some draft day decisions, such as taking Nylund third overall in 1982 ahead of future Hall of Famers Scott Stevens and Phil Housley. But in his view the impediments to progress weren't his precious picks. It was finding the right coach. That was a losing battle when it came to Ballard, especially when McNamara wanted John Brophy bounced.

"Whenever I brought [Brophy's future] up, Mr. Ballard said, 'Don't worry about it.' Some people would say, 'How could you [tolerate] that?' Well, I loved my job, loved where I was at, I loved the money. I was not about to tell him, 'I disagree. I quit.' But what we needed at that time was someone who could teach."

Gord Stellick had the job after McNamara for a year and half. Armed with lofty ideals, the 30-year-old wanted to make a difference, but by then just about everyone connected to the team was running for cover. "The sad part of it is, no one wants to talk about the '80s now," Vaive said. "Even for the guys that worked so hard during that period. Myself, the first 50-goal scorer on the team, Borje, still an All-Star at that time, Wendel's rookie campaign, Ihnacak's 30-goal year…we could put the puck in the net. We just couldn't keep it out. I never requested a trade, though there were a lot of exasperating moments when I asked myself, *Why am I doing this?* I always thought someone will come in here, grab the bull by the horns, and make the right deals. I always believed it would happen one day."

Vaive, McGill, and Steve Thomas were eventually traded by McNamara to the Chicago Blackhawks for Ed Olcyk and Al Secord. It was the last big deal before being replaced by Stellick. "You just wonder what we would have looked like around the early 1990s if everyone stayed together," Vaive said.

* * *

Darryl Shannon was an impressionable young defenceman who was elated to be a second-round pick of the Leafs in 1986. Unfortunately, he arrived at that time when older players were protecting their own skins, not looking out for kids. "Here I was so excited to play for this famous team," said Shannon, who was born in nearby Barrie, Ontario. "Yet things were so bad. When I came up, I asked a veteran for some playing advice. He said, 'just go out, skate hard, and make sure your arms are flapping. It makes it look like you're working.' I can just see myself trying to sneak by with that today with Mike Babcock and all the video they have."

Another newcomer found himself rooming with loose cannon John Kordic. At least that's what he thought when he checked into a road hotel early in the afternoon with Kordic's luggage in the room but no sign of the belligerent winger. "So I went to bed, figuring there must have been a mistake, maybe John was in another room," said Kordic's roommate, who wished to remain anonymous. "But at about 1:00 AM, he bursts through the door, yelling about something, takes the old metal key you used to have at hotels, and whips it at the window, which breaks. Then he flops into bed. I spent the whole night wide awake under the covers worried about what he might do to me."

* * *

There were many players on the Leafs whose careers would have taken off had they been a successful team. Case in point was diminutive speedster Daryl Evans, now a commentator with the Los Angeles Kings. "It was the year we were playing Detroit in the playoffs," Evans said of 1987. "I was one of the Black Aces. Then, I had finally got an opportunity to play, and we won at the Gardens and put us up 3–1 in the series. We were in Detroit for the next game with a chance to win. But toward the end of practice, I threw my back out. I was totally locked up, down on the ice, and couldn't move. Then Coach Brophy called everyone in to a corner of the rink for a meeting. I remember Paul Gardiner, our coach with the farm team in Newmarket, was helping run practice and I begged him, 'Paul, put your stick into the back of my pants and just push me into the pile. John was joking, 'Ha, one game and you think you can sit around.' But I really couldn't move. I told the trainers: please don't say anything to John and I got back to the hotel and did all my treatments. But I couldn't move next day either and never played another game in the NHL after that. What was even more unfortunate: we ended up losing that series [one of the few times an NHL club has come back from a 3–1 deficit]. The team that was waiting to play the winner of the series was the Oilers, and the reporters were saying that was why I'd been called up because I had success against them earlier and I'd have played against them again."

*　*　*

McNamara was hopeful of duplicating his scouting success with Salming in the autumn of 1985. He'd been told by Ballard to help with the defection of Miroslav Ihnacak, younger brother of Peter and one of a small band of Czechoslovakians who'd fled and found their way to the Leafs. The elder Ihnacak, Miroslav Frycer, and Marian Stastny (of the famous clan who'd made their way through the Iron Curtain to join the WHA's Quebec Nordiques) were among the top 10 in Leafs scoring in 1985–86 and held some sway with Ballard.

Ihnacak, who had 66 points for his club team the year before, was a late-round Leafs pick and a gamble in case he ever got out of the country. Having never seen him actually suit up, McNamara was wary of committing time, resources, and money to spring him. "But those [Czechs] are whispering in Mr. Ballard's ear, and he kept telling me, 'The guys say he can play,'" McNamara said.

McNamara secretly departed for Europe during the Christmas holidays, and immediately the trip seemed cursed. He and his secret go-between were delayed getting to Vienna, where an intermediary was to help Ihnacak pull off his escape. McNamara's plane arrived the day Palestinian terrorists shot up Vienna's airport, and they were re-routed. After hearing nothing all day, a message got through that Ihnacak was indeed "over the wall" but had complicated matters by bringing out a girl with him. "They threw a curve at me," McNamara said. "I was told [by the Czech contact] I had to pay for her [release], too."

McNamara refused to budge on the $150,000 limit Ballard had authorized for Ihnacak. Eventually he was given custody. "The Canadian consulate [in Vienna] then became my biggest problem," McNamara said. "They wanted to put Miro in a refugee camp right away."

McNamara felt he couldn't tell the consulate officials the back story of how Ihnacak happened to land right in his lap in case they wouldn't cooperate or help cut through the red tape with the Leafs. Eventually, McNamara called home to a high school friend from St. Michael's College, who worked in prime minister Brian Mulroney's office, reaching him at a New Year's Eve party.

It was agreed the government would assist McNamara with getting his prized catch out of Vienna without fuss. But there was the not-so-trifling matter of paying off the middlemen, who demanded their money in cash. "I went to the bank in Vienna to pay the guy who had come over with me and the guy who had brought Ihnacak out," McNamara said. "The bag they gave me with the money was transparent, so you could see all the bills. The Iron Curtain was still up,

Vienna was full of thieves and spies, and I'm walking around with all this money. Then these guys start arguing about their share. I finally said, 'Would you two shut up?' We ducked into a hotel, and I paid them, including some small bills, because the bank had stuffed all the cash they had into the bag."

A cover tale was concocted that Ihnacak had defected through Italy in the back of a truck. Stuck at the embassy another couple of days, the entire party was finally placed on a flight to London. McNamara said: "As we boarded, the woman from the embassy, who was assigned to help us, gave me a big hug and said, 'Don't ever do this again.'"

Naturally there was great fanfare at home when news broke of the Ihnacak caper. Yet McNamara had buyers' remorse immediately after Ihnacak practiced for the first time at Maple Leaf Gardens. He was not as big as projected, and his skating needed obvious work. "I mentioned right away to Gord Stellick," McNamara said, "'We're in trouble.'"

Fifty-five games, two seasons, and 17 points later, it was over for the player fans dubbed "Miro The Zero." "He was a nice kid," McNamara said upon reflection. "He was happy to get out, and I think he got about $100,000 in his contract. Maybe he didn't have a chance with us, but I was disappointed in his skating. If I'd seen him over there, I'd have talked Mr. Ballard out of it. But you cross him once, and he's got a memory like an elephant."

* * *

Consolation prizes for the Leafs' difficult years under McNamara did provide Toronto with a string of top 10 draft years. As a scout he was proud of Courtnall, Iafrate, Clark, and Damphousse. There also seemed to be stability behind the bench with Dan Maloney. After taking the job and being too iron-fisted with many veteran Leafs he considered too pampered, Maloney began his second year in 1985–86 on much better terms.

Despite a fourth-place finish in the Norris Division, Toronto upset a much better Chicago Blackhawks team in the first round, sweeping the best-of-five series. In Game 3 against Chicago with the Gardens filled with the so-called "real fans" who snapped up unclaimed postseason tickets from doubting subscribers, the place was electric. Denis Savard was hit by a fan's broom as the stunned Blackhawks exited. The Leafs then stretched the St. Louis Blues to seven games in the division final. Quite reasonably, Maloney requested a new three-year contract in the offseason, though Ballard urged McNamara not to offer more than one. Deeply insulted, but figuring he could take the Leafs even further the next season to justify a bigger raise, Maloney was going to say yes. But in a car ride back from Ballard's cottage—one of McNamara's rather menial chores was driving the big boss around—Ballard blurted out: "Gerry, ya know that contract for Maloney? Keep it in your pocket. I want John Brophy."

Ballard had become enamoured with tales of Brophy's old-school, Conn Smythe, beat-'em-in-the-alley values from his minor league days, his time as a Leafs assistant, then head coach of their AHL farm team down the road in St. Catharines. But from what McNamara had seen of Brophy, he was far too roguish. The GM stalled for time, asking Ballard for a chance to get to know Brophy better at the AHL meetings in Hilton Head, South Carolina.

McNamara's plane had barely landed there when a news photographer from a Toronto paper came up to ask him where Brophy was. When the suspicious McNamara asked why, the photographer said, 'oh, you didn't know? He's just been named coach of the Leafs.'"

Maloney was cut loose and found his way to the Winnipeg Jets, where he found some success, but he and the Leafs never recovered that playoff momentum. "I loved Dan," said Chris Kotsopoulos, a defenceman on that team. "I struggled the first few weeks after getting traded from Hartford because of lack of conditioning. He saw that I wasn't ready and worked with me. He believed in me, he trusted me, and I eventually had one of my best years. He was a players' coach who was just starting to blossom. A big mistake by Harold—and everyone knows the rest of the story."

* * *

Brophy came to Ballard's attention through his work as assistant coach, but he was too similar in temperament to headmaster Maloney. So in 1985–86, he was placed in charge of St. Catharines, an hour down the Queen Elizabeth Way. It became Brophy's private gulag where his old-school methods and survival of the fittest was the rule.

Incensed after one home loss, Brophy charged into the room and declared the players weren't going anywhere. He gave orders to send their wives and girlfriends home, cleared the rink, told the trainers to get out the practice jerseys, and bag-skated the whole lot. Another Saint remembered a loss in Sherbrooke where a smaller French Canadian player had showed him up. He gave the fellow a hard two-hander on his helmet for retaliation of a poor show of discipline, but Brophy endorsed the move.

The Saints were quite a crew. Kevin Maguire had 161 penalty minutes, but he was topped by Val James' 162, Chris McRae's 233, and Leigh Verstraete's 300. Todd Gill, Jeff Jackson, and Bill Kitchen were all around 100. Maguire, Muni, and McRae often found themselves in line brawls. Brophy often encouraged James to hang around the opposing dressing room before a game with his shift off and just flex his huge muscles.

When away from the rink, Brophy was a sharp dressed man. When he saw any suit or jacket he liked, he simply had to have it. In one home game, a Saints player suffered a leg injury and had to be taken to a hospital. There was certainly a great deal of concern as team staff, friends, and family escorted him. Seeing the player's coat left at the rink, Brophy tried it on and claimed ownership. The problem was that the player's wallet was still in there, and the team was going on a long road trip.

With the Maple Leafs, Brophy was sitting on the team bus one day in Chicago outside the posh Drake Hotel about five minutes before its departure to the old Chicago Stadium. He spotted another jacket he liked in the window of an upscale men's store, hopped out, paid more than $1,000 on the spot and re-boarded, proudly wearing it. When he showed up one night during playoffs behind the bench sporting a black fedora, looking like a mobster, he inspired a fan fashion trend right across the city.

Brophy considered himself very fortunate to have been given an NHL chance so late in his career and was determined to drive a message into his players: don't take such a privilege for granted. He told playmaking winger Frycer, a three-time 20-goal scorer, to "cut out that European crap" of carrying the puck over the blue line and demanded he adopt the standard North American dump and chase. He made Frycer work on a punching bag after practice, hoping to encourage him to fight. Later while bag-skating a group of Leafs, he would swing his stick at them as they came by to prod them, once striking Frycer so hard he re-injured his knee.

When a pudgy Iafrate showed up for camp about 15 pounds overweight, Brophy set up an exercise bike right in the team sauna. Only allowing Iafrate to take off his gloves and his skates, he left him to pedal away the pounds. "Poor Al," said McGill of the spectacle. "Then he goes out in a game and gets drilled by Sean McKenna of the Sabres in a fight. He hit Al so hard in the jaw he couldn't eat solid food for days, and that's how he lost the last of the 15 pounds."

But on a young squad that needed lessons—not the lash—Brophy's hard-line methods were not effective, particularly with McNamara's coddled draft picks, most of whom had been handed starting jobs. A huge chasm formed between them, Brophy, and some veterans. McNamara decried the working conditions of the young Leafs to Ballard. "I diss very few people. But if I was a Leafs player then, I'd have sued the Gardens," McNamara said. "Brophy set back about four players, guys who could play such as Courtnall, Damphousse, Iafrate, and Leeman. They hated him with a passion. I went to Mr. Ballard and said, 'You have to get rid of John.' But he said, 'He's coach, and you better learn to get along.' You'd wondered what this guy was teaching them, but Mr. Ballard liked stories about John, how he'd break the windows on the team bus because he was mad about a loss. I couldn't talk to Brophy. But he had a great relationship with the press. That's what kept him going, but it hurt the Leafs."

When the dressing room crisis was at its worst, Ballard was distracted by a battle for control of Gardens ownership with rivals and his own family. On one occasion with the Leafs struggling in the standings, McNamara thought he had support from Ballard to fire Brophy, but the boss went incommunicado at the last minute to avoid the confrontation. "The rest is history," McNamara said with a sigh. "I got fired. I'll take [the consequences] for the guys I drafted but not the won-loss record because I was saddled with a coach who couldn't win for losing."

* * *

In the autumn of 2013, bygones were bygones with Brophy's former Leafs. Many were on a travelling NHL alumni tour in Nova Scotia, where Brophy was in a retirement home.

"We had just got outside the [First Nations] reserve in Eskasoni," Mark Osborne said. "Guys such as Iafrate, Tom Fergus, Leeman, myself, Daoust. We had a long drive to our next game in Liverpool. We looked at the atlas and saw the road ran right through Antigonish. I'd got an earlier text message from [ex-Leafs player] Wes Jarvis, who reminded me John was in a nursing home there."

Osborne got directions and asked the bus driver to pull in for a surprise visit. "It was a series of cottages near a field with sheep running around," Osborne said of the unlikely setting for the gritty Brophy. "As soon as we went in, he just lit up, he was just tickled. We reminded him who everyone was. The funny thing was his unit had five elderly women. He kept on telling them he once coached the Leafs, and they didn't believe him. They'd say, 'Oh, sure you did John.'"

The Leafs all reminisced about a night Iafrate was on for the first shift of the game and was a minus-two right away. "Broph wanted him off the ice and kept yelling in that high-pitched voice of his: 'I-a-fray-tee!' while Garry Lariviere, his assistant, tried to settle him down," Osborne said. "John benched Al about 10 minutes and then put him back. Then Al goes minus-three, and we're down 3–0 after one period. None of us were really playing well that night, so we come off, and John yells, 'It's like you guys are playing in the dark, so sit in the dark.' And he shuts the dressing room lights off, left the room, and slammed the door. There we are: NHL players in complete darkness. Borje Salming finally said, 'Come on guys, turn on the lights.' Al was right by the switch, but Broph was listening outside. As soon as Al turned them on, he burst right through the door and screamed at him again. Then he started on Al's hair: 'I-a-fray-tee, you're bald, you're bald, you're bald.' You talk to all the players from his generation, the '70s and '80s, and they say there's nobody like Broph. The antics, his one-liners, the things he'd do between periods were unprecedented. And surviving the minor leagues with all those tough guys, he was such a competitive person. One year *Hockey Night in Canada* did a music feature 'The 12 Days Of Christmas.' The 10th day was 10 Brophy tantrums, and in each verse, the clip was him turning purple."

Brophy died in 2016 at age 83.

* * *

Had he been able to convince Ballard to make a coaching change from Brophy, McNamara claimed there were numerous candidates under consideration. One was former Leafs defenceman Quinn, who at the time working on a law degree in the U.S. after coaching the Philadelphia Flyers. McNamara and Quinn had been brief Leafs teammates in 1969–70, when McNamara filled in as a goalie.

McNamara was about 10 years ahead of his time, as Quinn became Toronto's coach in 1998 after furthering his career with the Vancouver Canucks. Ballard, however, didn't see a fit with Quinn at the time. McNamara also thought highly of an unknown Providence College coach named Lou Lamoriello, who was garnering lots of attention after success in the NCAA ranks with the Friars. McNamara had acquired Rich Costello, one of Lamoriello's former players, as part of the 1982 Sittler trade with Philadelphia. When the time came for Costello to leave the NCAA and sign with the Leafs, Lamoriello acted as his advisor. "I'd had a relationship with Lou, but Harold said, 'I don't want any college guy in here [so soon after Roger Nielson].' That was the end of Lamoriello."

He, too, would come around to join the Leafs, albeit not until 2015, staying three years as general manager.

Forgotten Man

Peter DeBoer, now the coach of the San Jose Sharks, will admit to a soft spot for the Leafs, who drafted him and Windsor Spitfires teammate Peter Ing in 1988. DeBoer, once a 91-point forward, doesn't blame anyone for not remembering his name in the 12th round, 237th overall long after the hoopla for the top Leafs picks that year, Scott Pearson, Tie Domi, and Ing.

"They don't even have 12 rounds anymore," DeBoer said, laughing. "I ended up still being in the rink [when called]. Dick Duff and Brophy were at the table. But it was last call at the bar on Sainte-Catherine Street, and I got out in time for a beer to celebrate."

Fletcher wasn't known as the Silver Fox for nothing. He pulled some incredible trades, including a record 10-player swap with the Flames. That was his modus operendi to rebuild the Leafs in the early '90s. Ken Daniels of CBLT went to Fletcher one day in the Leafs room to ask about rumours the Pittsburgh Penguins had approached him with an offer of a first and second-round pick to get Clark. "Draft, schmaft," retorted Fletcher, a quip he probably wanted to rescind not long after when a series of his trades for veterans that surrendered such assets did not result in a Cup and left the cupboard bare for many years.

Dave Andreychuk was the last Leafs player to achieve 50 goals to date (53 in '93–94) and scored many of them right in front of the net. He's in the Hall of Fame with another Leafs teammate, Glenn Anderson. But Anderson doesn't know how anyone could've neutralized the giant Andreychuk, who didn't just have the size but a gift for tipping pucks with his long reach.

"Can you imagine trying to move that body out?" Anderson said of what defencemen and goalies were faced with. "He made his living there. Basically, you're in a [small] kitchen and you've got 20 other people, trying to get you out. His hand-eye coordination is still there. He could tip any puck any time."

* * *

As he departed the Gardens in his daily practice and game night routine in the early '90s, winger Mike Foligno often encountered the same homeless person with hat in hand on the street. Foligno would give him a buck or two, and they had a regular rapport. One night Foligno and wife, Janis, were out for dinner near the Gardens and encountered the same man. As Foligno was in a bit of a hurry and had no small bills at the time, he promised to give the guy something when he left the restaurant. After their meal the man was still there, Foligno dug in his pocket and gave a few dollars, and the couple walked toward their parking spot. They were a few blocks away when the man rushed up, calling to Foligno. "I don't think you meant to give me this," he said, handing Foligno back his gold wedding ring that had accidentally slipped off his finger and into his hat.

He nearly forgot his ring, but the Foligno family will never forget Christmas of '91 in Toronto and what happened in the last game before the NHL's holiday break. While the Leafs had played four games in six nights, concluding with a December 23 home encounter against the Jets, Janis had busied herself wrapping gifts and getting the car packed for her husband and their four kids (including future

NHLers Marcus and Nick) to travel to his hometown of Sudbury. They were slated to leave right after the match and be up north in time to surprise relatives for Christmas Eve. With so much to do, Janis skipped attending that night's game, only tuning in to catch the score. "The first thing she heard about my broken leg was the announcer saying, 'Foligno has suffered a career-ending injury.' Talk about scary," Foligno said.

He had collided with Luciano Borsato of the Jets, and the worst was feared when he arrived at hospital. The tibia and fibula were both a mess. Pieces of bone were coming up through the skin and his hockey sock. As Christmas Eve arrived, a devastated Foligno was indeed in fear he'd played his last game at age 32. What happened next was like something out of the holiday classic *It's A Wonderful Life*.

First to arrive after his surgery were assistant coaches Mike Murphy and Mike Kitchen, bearing a basket of fruit and the gag gift of adult magazines. They were followed by Fletcher with a bottle of wine and a cheese tray. Teammate Peter Zezel's mother baked cookies, and chairman of the board Steve Stavro came by. Coach Tom Watt arrived in a Santa Claus suit to entertain the kids. Bob Rouse's wife, Dianne, helped Janis prepare a turkey dinner for Christmas Day, which the whole family ate around his bed. "We made the best of a bad situation, but that's just the type of people we are," Foligno said.

Even the Foligno family reunion was rescued when the Leafs flew Foligno's mother down from Sudbury. "I can't tell you how much that affected me," Foligno said. "Everybody from top to bottom in the organization took an interest. That was as much an inspiration as anything to get better."

He did come back to play, rollerblading in the spring, skating by August, and scoring in overtime in the next season's playoffs against Detroit. His knee was sound enough to perform his familiar celebratory goal jump.

Foligno became resigned to something chaotic happening every Christmas. It was just before Christmas 1990 that he was shocked to be told his 10 years as a Buffalo Sabre were done in a trade to the Leafs. Janis and the kids were just going out the door to the Sabres' family holiday party. "I told her not to bother. We're going to the Leafs' Christmas party instead," Foligno said.

A few years earlier, the Folignos had another Christmas trip planned for Sudbury. But that was only accomplished by getting through a series of blizzard conditions that began in Buffalo. Visibility was so limited at times that Janis had to roll down the side window to help navigate for his driving. During another yuletide they put an impressive 12-foot Christmas tree in the front foyer of their Buffalo house. He took note that it didn't look 100 percent stable in the stand, but they decorated it anyway, and he went off to a road game. "I got a call at 6:30 AM," Foligno said. "The tree was down, water was all over the place, and a lot of the balls were broken."

* * *

Nick Beverley found himself in an unlikely position in March of 1996: behind the Leafs bench. The director of pro scouting was the emergency replacement for Burns when the latter left the team, giving Beverly little time to reorganize for a home game against New Jersey. "Right off the bat, we had too many men on the ice," Beverly said. "The linesman took pity on us and didn't call it, so we quietly tried to pull our extra guy off until Mike Craig skates right past the benches, yelling out loud, 'We've got too many out here,' but he keeps going. The linesman just looks at me and rolls his eyes."

Beverly kept the Leafs on course for the playoffs, and the team finished with a record of 9–6–2. They faced the St. Louis Blues in the first round and played a particular stinker on the road. Beverly said he pulled starter Felix Potvin after two periods "to wake up the rest of the nimrods" on his team. Nimrod was old schoolyard slang in Toronto for an idiot, but feeling bad about his choice of words, Beverly insisted he was using the biblical reference of Nimrod the mighty hunter and challenged the media to look it up. "I was losing my mind after the game, and Nimrod just came out," Beverly said. "Nimrod is good. I just meant it sarcastically. Then it became a big story."

Jack of All Trades

Todd Gill played more than 700 regular season and playoff games for the Leafs between 1984 and 1996 and thus saw his share of trades. In the Fletcher era, 51 deals were made from the latter's arrival to the one that sent Gill to the San Jose Sharks for Jamie Baker. Gill lost three roommates—Randy Wood, Ken Wregget, and Clark—to trades, while the Gardens dressing room stall next to Gill's became known as a black hole that claimed Rouse, Tom Kurvers, Rob Ramage, and Sylvain Lefebvre. Gill did his best to alleviate the shock for each man who received the dreaded notice he was leaving. "After every trade I call the guy, but I still get uncomfortable," Gill said. "You tell them, 'You've got a friend for life' and you wish them good luck, but it's not an easy thing to do."

CHAPTER 10
ONE-LINERS

A collection of Maple Leafs zingers:

"If you can't beat 'em in the alley, you can't beat 'em on the ice."
—Conn Smythe on creating a tough team to beat clubs
such as the Montreal Canadiens

"The Leafs are playing as ragged as a hobo's jacket."
—Broadcaster Danny Gallivan

"Those Penguins are done like dinner."
—Tiger Williams when the Leafs went ahead in a 1977 playoff
series against the Pittsburgh Penguins

"Everyone was put on Earth for a purpose. Mine is to sell newspapers."
—Eric Lindros

"You could tell they were big shooters. They came in through the Carlton St. doors."
—Jim McKenny, then a Marborough junior and part-time
Maple Leaf Gardens worker, when he saw The Beatles arrive
for a concert in 1964

"Daddy's home!"
—Ken Baumgartner's favourite line
when jumping into a fight

"Playing the Leafs is like eating Chinese food. An hour later, you want to play them again."
—Coach-turned-commentator Roger Neilson
on the sad state of his old team in the early '80s

"I think he's from Afghanistan, Tajikastan...one of the Stans."
—Coach Pat Quinn, trying to recall the Khazikstan
homeland of winger Nik Antropov

The immaculately dressed Conn Smythe, who leaves the Leafs' dressing room in 1937, advocated a "beat-'em-in-the-alley" attitude.

"Let me see your knuckles, kid!"

—*Coach John Brophy at the Leafs draft table in 1988*
in his first meeting with top pick Scott Pearson

"Fans didn't live here like I did, but they did in their dreams."

—*Paul Morris, public-address announcer,*
on the night The Gardens closed in 1999

"It's clear fans will stick with the Leafs, thick and thin, even though it has mostly been thin."

—*Former Toronto Toro Rick Foley on why his more successful*
WHA team could not win the city's heart

"The last time I got a ring from anyone, it was 45 years ago when I got married. I hope this one lasts as long."

—*Ex-Leafs player Frank Mathers after receiving his Hall*
of Fame ring in 1992 when elected to the builders' wing

"You're like a bunch of sheep. Baaah, baaah."

—*Quinn's description of the Toronto media chasing a story*

"Bob McGill's stick is not exactly the best example of advanced weaponry."

—*Mike Keenan on the low scoring defenceman,*
who played for both the Leafs and Keenan's Chicago Blackhawks

"Let's have one more. We'll sleep better."

—*Bert Olmstead to Leafs teammates at a bar in Chicago*
the night before a Stanley Cup playoff game in 1962

"There's more heat on me than Ted Bundy."

—*Gord Stellick in his final days as general manager*

"I fill when empty, empty when filled, and scratch when it itches."

—General manager Lou Lamoriello
on his management philosophy

"Nice broads and anything adverse to what a human being should do."

—Harold Ballard on how he lived into his 80s

"We couldn't find the net with a Norden bomb sight."

—World War II buff Quinn on his team's poor shooting
in a playoff game

"This is not so much a case of prizes being up for grabs as grabs being the prizes."

—Toronto Evening Telegram writer Bob Pennington
on the thin list of players the Leafs and other Original Six teams left
for the '67 expansion clubs to draft

"A blind man could see we didn't play well tonight."

—Coach Doug Carpenter after a galling loss

"Do what you do best: don't try and impress me by beating up someone."

—Pat Burns' advice for new players at training camp

"If we don't get rid of these fucking Czechs, we're going nowhere."

—Colour commentator Bill Watters caught on radio
with a live microphone when three Czech-born Leafs
were putting in a weak effort

"This is how I look at it. They hired me to decide. I'm just going to keep on keepin' on. If you let the noise get in the way...can you imagine if every time someone in your life told you that 'you couldn't do it,' you listened to them? Where would you be?"

—Coach Mike Babcock on facing critics

"He wants the best and expects the best. You can call that stubborn if you want."

—Patrick Marleau on Babcock

"Just like a bar in Kelvington on a Saturday night."

—Saskatchewan small towner Wendel Clark
after a massive brawl involving the Leafs and Detroit Red Wings
in his rookie season

"He wanted no one bigger than himself, and it killed that franchise."

—Paul Henderson on Ballard's headline grabbing

"He felt so bad after that game that he jumped in front of a subway train, but it went right between his legs."

—Darryl Sittler on Boston Bruins goalie Dave Reece,
the victim on his 10-point night

"Sometimes, I think we should just call them the Toronto White Knights."

—Scotty Bowman after coaching a game against the Leafs
where he felt the referees were reluctant to make calls
against "Canada's team"

"I'm through signing leases."

—Centre Dave McLlwain after joining the Leafs, his fourth
team that season, late in the 1991–92 schedule

"It's 70 miles there, but 70,000 miles back."

—John Brophy's frequent warning to laggard Leafs that they
would be sent to the St. Catherines farm team

"The man had maple syrup in his veins."

—Brian Conacher on '67 Cup teammate Dave Keon

"There was a couple doing the wild thing up in a private box the other night. They even brought a pillow. I guess they wanted to say they were the last to do it in the Gardens."

—An usher on what he witnessed as the famous rink closed to
NHL hockey

"It was like hiding paintings from the Nazis."

—A Gardens worker on saving some Leafs artifacts Ballard
had designated for trash

"The fat is in the fire."

—Rex MacLeod of the Toronto Star's *proposed lede*
after Ballard's death

"He was pre-deceased by his hockey team."

—MacLeod's proposed ending of the obit

"No finer person, teammate, or hockey player ever lived."

—George Armstrong on Tim Horton

"He was a handful. When he drank, everybody drank. When he told a joke, everybody laughed. The best thing to do when he got pissed was to stay out of his way."

—Eddie Shack on Horton

"If it was easy, if it was fair, everyone would win the Cup every 30 years. The good franchises don't think like that—they want to win it every year. If you manage it right, draft right, develop right, you'll be good a long time."

—Babcock on the Leafs' long-range picture

"He was a better player than me, but I'm more well known."

—Armstrong on the late Tod Sloan, a cousin of Keon's
and a fellow Northern Ontarian

"There are NHL rules, and there are Tie Domi rules."

—Domi, the Leafs' penalty king on his frequent suspensions

"In Montreal you're stupid twice [in two languages]. In Toronto you're only stupid once, but you're stupid a lot."

> —*Brian Burke on the difference of being general manager in Canada's two hottest hockey media and fan hotbeds*

"I've taken paycheques from teams, from TV outlets, cable companies, but always say I work for the fans. If they don't like what I do, I'm not working."

> —*Former Leafs broadcaster Jiggs McDonald*

"They must really need the money here."

> —*Leafs defenceman Dmitri Yushkevich, who was surprised to see board advertising at Nassau Coliseum on Long Island for Aeroflot, his much-maligned home country airline*

"I just consider it 'combat pay.'"

> —*Coach Ron Wilson, justifying a raise he was given in the midst of a difficult season when he was under heavy public scrutiny*

"We've had the glowing puck, so why not one that can set off sparks and a goal light when it crosses the line?"

> —*Play-by-play man Joe Bowen on NHL gimmicks*

"In 20 years I might be the only survivor left from that night. We didn't think much about it because we thought there would be more."

> —*Hockey Night in Canada's Brian McFarlane on sneaking into the last Leafs team's Stanley Cup party at executive Stafford Smythe's house in 1967*

"The Blue Jays and other teams are just renting this town. The Leafs still own it."

> —*Former Gardens superintendent Wayne Gillespie*

CHAPTER 11
FAN-DEMONIUM

Since the 1930s Toronto fans have wanted to dress just like the Maple Leafs—whether it was buying a replica sweater through the Eaton's department store (whose thick catalogues were said to have made great shin guards or goal pads) or having Mom sew or knit something resembling the blue and white logo.

On February 19, 1962, a new fashion statement was created when twistin' musician Chubby Checker became the first to wear a Leafs sweater on stage. He'd asked to borrow the jersey for the night, and, though former public relations man Stan Obodiac humourously noted Checker "forgot" to return it, a tradition was born. Until the closing of the Gardens in 1999, performers from ABBA to ZZ Top were given Leaf sweaters as welcoming gifts. The Who, The Eagles, Queen's Freddie Mercury, and Linda Ronstandt wore theirs while performing.

Many people have posted pictures of the Leafs sweater on display in the ABBA museum in Sweden. It's from one of the group's many appearances at the Gardens. Pete Townshend of The Who, a group that made multiple visits to the venue, was given a Leafs satin jacket, which he often wore while travelling.

Sales shot up in 1998 when Toronto blended the Ballard Leaf logo with vintage leafs on the sleeves. The team even received a phone call from England, where retired rocker Dave Clark of the Dave Clark Five wanted a brand new model because the one given him in the mid-1960s, which he'd worn for years during gardening around his estate, had become too faded.

Inside the current Leafs room are the Tragically Hip's hand-written lyrics to "Fifty Mission Cap," the Kingston-based band's ode to 1951 Cup overtime hero Bill Barilko. That 1993 release, still played at home games, was a favourite of coach Pat Burns that season and many of his players. The Leafs had not won the Cup for the 11 years that Barilko's body lay undiscovered after a crash in Northern Ontario, but afterward they won four Cups in the 1960s. Burns' team was coming close to a near worst-to-first turnaround, and the song was particularly powerful that season.

That aura returned in 2017 when the Hip's lead singer, Gord Downie, passed away after a brave battle with cancer. He performed on stage until near the end. Defenceman Morgan Rielly and the Leafs picked out a couple of Hip tunes to play in the dressing room the day after Downie's death. "He was a huge inspiration to all of Canada," Rielly said. "We have a lot of fans of him in this room. All over Toronto, all over Canada, and the world, losing him is tough. I like the song, 'New Orleans Is Sinking, Ahead by a Century'… they're all classics. And I've heard the Barilko story a few times." Connor Brown said he was a fan and recalls his parents played a lot of Hip albums in the family home.

Ben Smith has quite the connections in the music and entertainment worlds. The captain of the 2018 Calder Cup champion Toronto Marlies is the son of Larry Alan Smith, a noted composer in the U.S., and Marguerita Oundjian-Smith, a pianist and chambre musician. Smith's uncle, Peter Oundjian, was a musical director of the Toronto Symphony, and his cousin is Eric Idle, of Monty Python fame.

His father hitched a ride on the Chicago Blackhawks' open top team bus when they won the 2013 Cup and came through the Windy City on parade. Larry recorded some audio of the crowd noise bouncing off tall buildings for use in a future composition. Oundjian, meanwhile, became a big Marlies fan and attended some games live. Idle knows the least about hockey but keeps his 400,000 Twitter followers up to date on Ben's exploits. "Eric's a first cousin of my mom," Smith explained. "She was born in Toronto but went back to the U.K. when she was seven. I hear from Eric a couple of times a year. It's amazing to see his stardom. I might not have fully appreciated it until I met him. A couple of times he came to a game when [the Blackhawks] were playing in Los Angeles. People were just so excited to see him. I didn't quite understand he was a pretty big celebrity. Now, I see what they go through."

Idle was the force behind the Broadway play *Spamalot*, which Smith attended with family in 2005. "It's fun to see him in movies and TV," Smith said. "[The humour] is a little lost on me, but my Mom and her siblings are big fans."

When the Leafs and Los Angeles Kings met in the 1993 conference final, and the venue switched to Tinseltown, one of the advantages of the extended stay near the bright lights of Hollywood for Toronto was casual interaction with plenty of stars. "Michael Keaton stopped and wished our players good luck in a restaurant," Pat Park said. "And I saw Courteney Cox."

Bill Berg's brushes with greatness on that trip included Robert Loggia from the Tom Hanks' movie *Big*, as well as Julianne Phillips, the first wife of Bruce Springsteen. Scouting director Pierre Dorion recognized Canadian-born Michael J. Fox. During a hotel pool/patio party at their team hotel, Loews Santa Monica, the Leafs walked through a crowd that included veteran actor Lloyd Bridges; his equally well-known sons, Jeff and Beau; Bernie Koppel (Siegfried from *Get Smart* and Doc from *Love Boat*); and a couple of TV game-show hosts. "I held the elevator for the Bionic Woman [Lindsay Wagner]," Bob Stellick joked. "We've seen Michelle Pfeifer out here and Gregory Hines."

Across the street from the hotel, Leafs brass frequented the famous hole-in-the-wall bar, Chez Jays. Frank Sinatra and Marlon Brando had frequented the place in the Rat Pack days, Richard Harris sang "MacArthur Park" there for the first time, astronaut Alan Shepard took one of the bar's peanuts to space—the "Astro-Nut" is in the current owner's safety deposit box somewhere—and Marilyn Monroe supposedly waited there for a rendezvous with John F. Kennedy.

The arrival of the Baby Leafs in Newfoundland during the '90s saw the Barenaked Ladies, Kim Mitchell, and other Canadian musical acts display the St. John's version of the Leafs sweater. Orders were already coming in during the summer of 2018 for the Newfoundland Growlers, the new ECHL affiliate first coached by native son Ryane Clowe. Mike Myers, David Letterman, Jay Baruchel, and Will Arnett have also been spotted with Leaf sweaters. Mitch Marner, a big fan of the film *Blades of Glory*, saw Arnett featured on the scoreboard during a home game and mentioned he'd like to meet the actor. "When he came and [spoke] to me, I got starstruck," Marner said.

"I didn't know how to say anything back. It was definitely one of the highlights of my life. I told my parents about it after, and they went absolutely bonkers."

In 1999 several Leafs were thrilled to see 76-year-old veteran actor Len Lesser (of *Seinfeld* and the war movie *Kelly's Heroes*) paraded through the Air Canada Centre room in his sweater to film an audience participation video. He was appearing in a play in town. "I like your work," he told goaltender Curtis Joseph.

"Just don't tell me to break a leg," Joseph quipped.

Lesser's favourite team was actually the Detroit Red Wings, even though he's from The Bronx. "I had a very perverse childhood," Lesser explained.

* * *

For years the entrance to the Leafs dressing room at the Gardens was one door, albeit a very thick wood that was varnished and painted many times from the building's 1932 opening to the Leafs' departure in '99. Before the building actually closed, however, a devious employee took it off its hinges and hid it in his garage. But it was too "hot" to hang on to—not to mention the guy's wife eventually became sick of it taking up so much room. So it was eventually sold to Ultimate Leafs Fan Mike Wilson, who made it the centrepiece of his team-themed museum.

The other access to the Leaf room on the Gardens' east side was off the main corridor at the coach's office. Sometimes, the media was let in that way rather than through the main dressing room, but the quarters became quite crowded once TV cameras became part of the postgame ritual.

One particularly busy night, John Brophy was surrounded at his desk and barely able to move. He and reporters noticed two inebriated fans had slipped in among the media mob and were eyeing his video recording equipment as a souvenir.

In the summer of 2018, Erik Blome, the Illinois-based sculptor of the Leafs Legends Row monument, dropped by on his annual maintenance visit to spruce up his statues after weather-related exposure. He noticed a group of black players in bright green and red sweaters posing with the Leafs greats and struck up a conversation. They were the Kenyan Ice Lions, the African country's first national team, who were in Canada to practice, see some hockey sites such as Scotiabank Arena, and meet NHL stars Sidney Crosby and Nathan MacKinnon. "I was in Kenya just two months [earlier]," said Blome, whose works include a statue of civil rights icon Rosa Parks in downtown Dallas. "I gave a talk on sculpture at the University of Nairobi through Fulbright. It turns out one of [the Kenyan players] had been to it. What a tiny world."

Two months later, the Leafs invited Ice Lions captain Benard Azegere to see the Leafs and Crosby's Pittsburgh Penguins and gave him a Leafs jersey.

It didn't take long for a discarded Mats Sundin stick to set off a price war among souvenir hunters at the Air Canada Centre in January of 2004. Angry at the way a shift was going and frustrated at breaking the shaft of his shillelagh, the Toronto captain flung it into the crowd, nearly striking Harriet and Arnold Kilbrick, a couple sitting 15 rows up in the golds. Contrite about his display of emotion, Sundin asked Leaf staffers to find whoever wound up with the busted stick and replace it with a new one, which he signed to emphasize his apology.

But the Kilbricks, casual hockey observers, weren't out of the rink when approached by numerous hard-core fans willing to pay good coin for such a prize. Before leaving they accepted $600 from Steve Silva, who was at the game with buddy Rob Cabral. Both were wearing their No. 13 Sundin sweaters. At last report someone called a Toronto radio station and offered Silva $4,500 for it.

* * *

A Weir Connection

It was strange to hear the entire Leafs dressing room talk about golf in the midst of playoffs, but that was the scene in their 2003 series against the Philadelphia Flyers. That's because Canadian Mike Weir won The Masters and had the whole country talking links. Weir was quickly ferried to Toronto for a special pregame ceremony. Among those happiest to see him was defenceman Ric Jackman, who'd drawn Weir's name in the dressing room pool.

"He is one of my favourite golfers, a good Canadian boy," Jackman said.

Pat Park, then the Leafs director of media relations, was proud to call Weir a neighbour. Bright's Grove is 10 minutes north of Park's hometown of Sarnia. "We always drive by the club he played at as a youngster, Huron Oaks," Park said. "They always have this sign out front: 'Home of Mike Weir' in very small letters. When I was growing up, you'd always see his picture in the *Sarnia Observer*, a kid winning some kind of golf award."

One of Tie Domi's most memorable scraps at the rink didn't involve a fellow NHLer.

In March of 2001 in a heated game against the Flyers at then–First Union Center, Domi was sent to the box for unsportsmanlike conduct after a disturbance with Luke Richardson. While Domi was doing his time, an oversized fan with beer in hand began berating him on the other side of the glass, making threatening gestures and leaning over the top. After Domi had heard enough, he grabbed a bottle of water and squirted it at him, but the guy pressed even closer. The glass gave way, and 35-year-old Chris Falcone tumbled into the box with Domi and the off-ice officials.

Not thinking of the consequences, Domi seized the fan and started punching him relentlessly before security broke it up. "It was like watching someone fall into the lion's den at the zoo," chortled teammate Curtis Joseph.

Domi was eventually assessed a $1,000 fine by the NHL for his actions. "Squirting water was not right," he said. "I should have not

In response to a Philadelphia Flyers fan berating him, Tie Domi squirts him with water. A fight between them ensued.

lowered myself by responding with an action that brought me down to his level, but it was the only thing I could think of doing while being doused with beer."

The possibility of legal action remained despite what many thought was justifiable defence by Domi. Yet the two eventually settled the matter, which included Domi paying for Falcone and his family to come to Toronto to watch a couple of playoff games at the player's expense. "We solved it like two street guys," Domi explained to a Philly radio station. "No lawyers, no nothing. We shook on it. Everything is good now. I'm really glad it all worked out."

Domi enjoyed playing in front of the tough Philly crowd, whom he said respected his style of play. "The fan mail I get from the Philly fans is just incredible. It's more than any place in the whole league— to tell you the truth. I played it up in Philly, especially for the fans. They were on me, and I would kind of taunt them too, so it was a lot of fun."

*   *   *

As the Leafs warmed up for their last game of the 2014–15 season at home against Montreal, they wondered about the guy in the No. 30 Toronto sweater getting all the media attention up in the stands. He was Lindsay, Ontario-born businessman Rob Suggitt, and that night's game was completing a frenetic fund-raising challenge that saw him hit all 30 NHL rinks in 30 days (prior to Las Vegas joining the league). "I didn't even know it was possible until I mapped it out," Suggitt said. "I'd talked about this with friends and family for 10 years, but time and cost always got in the way."

Suggitt's Edmonton-based magazine publishing company footed the bill so he could raise $30,000 for the Children's Make-A-Wish foundation. The 53-year-old had begun his quest a month earlier at Nassau Coliseum on Long Island for the New York Islanders-Ottawa Senators game. He was so pleased that a Leafs-Montreal Canadians tilt, a match-up of the league's two oldest rivals, would be last game, though in his travels he encountered the Red Wings as the visitors five times.

He nearly missed stop No. 29 in Columbus, Ohio, when a connecting flight from Montreal was stranded in Toronto for maintenance. He barely made it to Ohio and then flew back to Toronto early the next morning for Leafs–Habs. In all, Suggitt criss-crossed the continent on 27 flights, two auto rentals, and one Amtrak rail trip between New York and Philadelphia.

Not all Southern Ontario kids grew up rooting for the Leafs. During the team's annual skills competition in 2000 at the Air Canada Centre, the Leafs allowed top minor hockey players in the area to participate and try some of the same events, such as target shooting and skating drills. A 10-year-old kid named Logan Couture from Lucan, Ontario, near London, stole the show, got to meet Mats Sundin and Sergei Berezin, and would later become an NHL star with the San Jose Sharks. "I still have that trophy in my room," said Couture, who grew up a Buffalo

Sabres fan, at the 2016 World Cup. "It has a big Leaf on it, even though the Leafs were not my team. So that was tough. It's great trophy, probably my best one, but I didn't like the Leaf thing on it."

*   *   *

In 1993 during the Blue Jays' second World Series run, slugger Joe Carter decided to relax midway through the American League Championship Series against the Chicago White Sox by taking in the Leafs' season opener against the Dallas Stars. With indoor pyrotechnics a fad in the NHL at the time, Carter was as impressed as anyone at the Gardens by the pregame fireworks that followed player introductions. But as Carter gazed at the smoke lingering above the ice, a cinder became lodged in his eye.

He tried to scratch it out, but that only caused more irritation. The Leafs summoned their team ophthalmologist, Michael Easterbrook, to examine Carter, and it was determined he should go to nearby Wellesley Hospital to make sure there was no infection. Bob Stellick felt responsible for the mishap as the pyro show was his idea, so he drove Carter and Easterbrook to the hospital in the second intermission. Stellick was panicking that he and the team would be lambasted if Carter missed any playoff time. "I was sweating; Joe was great," Stellick said. "The rest is history. Fortunately, Joe didn't hit his [World Series walk-off] home run with an eye patch."

CHAPTER 12
GO, GO GOALIES

Long before the era of masks, the first regular netminder for the Leafs wore only a baseball cap. It wasn't for warmth—but for protection from loogies. Harry Holmes was quite bald, and before there was glass or much in the way of fencing around the rink, fans got up close and personal. Holmes' shiny pate made a tempting target for fans trying to throw him off his game. As goalies of the day were discouraged from going down to make saves, people would spit or fire a wad of gum or chewing tobacco at Holmes, so he took to wearing the hat.

Born just outside of Toronto in Aurora, Holmes won a Stanley Cup with four different teams in the Pacific Coast Hockey Association and then the fledgling NHL. He had a laid-back style that contributed to his nickname of "Happy." Holmes was on the inaugural Toronto team in the 1917–18 NHL (known as the Arenas) and signed after the first game when Art Brooks and Sammy Herbert combined to give up 10 goals to the Montreal Wanderers. He was on the Toronto Cup team that season and won every year his team was in the final—except for 1919 when he went back west to play for the Seattle Metropolitans, whose championship series with the Montreal Canadiens had to be canceled by the post-war influenza epidemic.

With goalies allowed to flop to make saves as the 1920s began, "Jumpin" Jake Forbes was in net for the St. Patricks after their name change from the Arenas. Toronto native Forbes was noted for two things: taking delivery of the first set of Emil "Pops" Kenesky's custom made goal pads and becoming the first NHL player to sit out a whole year in a salary dispute with the Pats. Kenesky was a saddle maker down the road in Hamilton and fashioned cricket pads for Forbes. Everyone wanted Kenesky's, the official supplier to the NHL right up until the 1970s. Pops even made a pair that helped Johnny Bower's bowlegged condition.

Another early 20th century netminder, John Ross Roach played goal seven years for the franchise, including the first game as the Leafs on February 17, 1927. He rarely missed a start and holds the distinction of being the only Toronto goalie ever to captain the team, which occurred during 1924–25. Listed at 5'5", he was sometimes called upon to play

10 extra minutes, as sudden death overtime was not on the books until all extra-period games were discontinued after 1929–30.

* * *

During frigid Canadian Prairie winters in northern Saskatchewan, young Johnny Bower had a lot of ice and a lot of room to play hockey. But a slow skater and rather big for his age of 10, he noticed his friends getting knocked over and hacked and thought standing in net would be "easy as pie." However, the pucks (composed of dense wood or frozen cow manure) started bruising him. One day, Bower recalled a friend's dad had thrown out an old baby mattress. The players cut it in two and sewed the stuffing, creating crude goal pads for Bower, which were strapped on with elastic bands. Next came a poplar tree branch in the shape of a goal stick that Bower's dad spotted and cut down. Through those modest beginnings, Bower became a Hall of

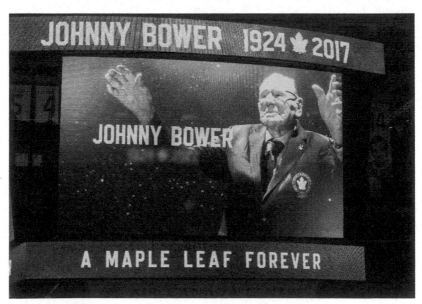

The Maple Leafs honour their former goalie, Johnny Bower, a Hall of Famer and four-time Stanley Cup winner, in 2018.

Famer, four-time Cup winner, and climbed to second in Leafs wins behind Turk Broda.

Few endured the pain Bower did for love of the game, their team, and its fans. "Johnny knew Toronto was a special place, having been in New York a while earlier," said Leafs teammate Dick Duff. "We weren't paid much but were always there, practices included. Bower and the goalies had it much harder. They had yellow and green bruises all the time and no mask. By the time they were aged 30, they looked 100. But we were respected by people in Canada. We were their entertainment—even if we didn't make a lot of money. Johnny knew if he didn't play well, there was a carload of goalies waiting to take his job."

* * *

Once Cliff Fletcher got to know Felix Potvin a little more (the goalie was drafted by predecessor Floyd Smith), they came around to talking about their shared background as residents in the Montreal area. It turned out Felix's father, Pierre, was a fireman whose station was very close to the Fletcher home. Potvin always kept a good luck medallion from his parents, which he kept on a clip inside his catcher's mitt.

Potvin's greatest moment outside the Leafs' crease was undoubtedly his November 10, 1996 brawl with Ron Hextall of the Philadelphia Flyers. Of course, goalies don't just fly down the ice and start a fight with each other. Their scrap developed with eight seconds remaining in one of those bad blood Flyers-Leafs game in Philly. With his team down 3–1, Toronto coach Mike Murphy felt the Flyers were planning to come after Doug Gilmour with the presence of Dan Kordic and Daniel Lacroix on the final faceoff.

Tie Domi came out to help Wendel Clark watch Gilmour's back, and Flyers coach Terry Murray countered with Scott Daniels, the orange and black's penalty minute leader, adding to the toxic mix. When Lacroix menaced Potvin, Clark started pounding on him, and Hextall, sensing it wasn't a fair fight, sprinted down, shedding his blocker and mitt, and had Potvin in his sights.

In what some Internet polls voted the best goalie fight of all time, the two exchanged a long sequence of haymakers. Hextall had a height advantage on Potvin, was seven years older, and was already well established as one of the league's most combative keepers. What he didn't know was Potvin's father had taught him a thing or two about defending himself. Detroit Red Wings coach Jacques Demers recalled Pierre Potvin was one of the strongest senior hockey players he met in the old days in Quebec, and it turned out Potvin's uncles were the toughest hombres in their neighbourhood. Hextall was cut in the dust-up, and the Flyers later claimed that Potvin must have head-butted him.

There was also plenty of fight in Mark LaForest. Though he didn't play behind a particularly strong Leafs team, he took exception to opposite number, Sean Burke, getting involved in a line brawl between Toronto and the New Jersey Devils at the Gardens on October 23, 1989. He skated the length of the ice to take on the bigger Burke and caught the worst of it, perhaps not knowing Burke was an accomplished boxer.

Almost 20 years later, LaForest found himself in a real combat zone—in Afghanistan. He was there voluntarily as the netminder for the Leafs/NHL alumni hockey team on a morale-building mission at the Kandahar Air Base housing Canadian and U.S. forces. Homesick troops had constructed a hockey rink in the middle of the desert. The heat could take a toll on players running about, and rolling around with several pounds of goalie equipment had extra challenges on a dehydrated body. But the gritty LaForest was a favourite among the service personnel, who let the NHL visitors ride in armoured vehicles and take part in military drills. The chain-smoking LaForest refused to butt out during the often intense games but once lost his cigarette somewhere inside his cage after taking a shot off the head. Spectators were treated to the sight of smoke coming out every air hole in his mask, as LaForest soldiered on.

Rick Wamsley's warfare was more psychological. In the early '90s, the backup Wamsley didn't get to play a lot behind Potvin and earlier

Grant Fuhr. But he contributed in any way possible. A superstitious warm-up ritual for many NHLers was to be the last player off the ice among both teams, which Auston Matthews and Mitch Marner continue to do with today's Leafs. Knowing that every team had players who were fixated about staying out or ending the skate by shooting a puck into an empty opposition net, Wamsley would stay in his goal long after other Leafs departed to prevent those shots and gain a perceived psychological advantage.

* * *

Rick St. Croix was one of the unfortunate Leafs goalies playing behind a weak blue line in 1984–85, a year in which the club gave up 358 goals and missed the playoffs. His season was also curtailed by a lower body muscle pull in a 5–3 home loss against the Boston Bruins. Leafs doctors decided he should be taken to hospital, and paramedics came out to place him on a stretcher in full equipment. The ambulance was closest to the centre ice exit, as opposed to the wide port for the Zamboni at the north end.

While the gate at the boards could be easily opened, the plexiglass could not be removed without some complications. The stretcher was at its lowest position, but there was still the risk of St. Croix's head not making it under the glass. "Several people eventually shared a brain," said Leafs photographer Graig Abel, "and the pane was removed so Rick could go through safely."

As Toronto's goalie coach in 2015, St. Croix was in the stands in Sunrise, Florida, when both Florida Panthers starters, Roberto Luongo and Al Montoya, were injured. Panthers goalie coach Robb Tallas, days away from his 42nd birthday, suited up just in case. St. Croix was asked if he would have put the equipment back on to help his team. He replied, "That's how people get heart attacks."

Back from the Bay

Finnish goalie Vesa Toskala's first game back in San Jose after his trade to the Leafs in 2007 naturally brought out a large media contingent. Talk came around to how hard it was to leave his longtime Bay Area residence and move so far away. Did he have to leave any pets behind?

"Four legs or two?" was Toskala's mischievous reply.

The likeable Toskala was quick with a one-liner but not so good on long shots. He was blamed for some awful goals from great distances, including a 197-foot clearing pass by Rob Davison that bounced about four times before eluding the Finn. Davison was a former San Jose Sharks teammate, who later was assistant coach of Toronto's farm team. When Toskala retired, the rumour was he took all his gear outside and set fire to it.

Goalie coach Steve Briere never played in the NHL but had quite a story to tell about his roundabout route to the Leafs. His first steady paying job in net was in Biloxi, Mississippi, with an East Coast Hockey League team called the Sea Wolves. His $500 weekly wage came down to $366 after taxes, and when he checked the fine print, the contract could be terminated for any reason with just 48 hours' notice.

He played on six different North American minor league teams between 1999 and 2002 and then tried his luck tending twine in Britain while putting an entrepreneurial degree at the University of Alabama-Huntsville to good use. Among the businesses he set up, using just a phone and computer, were a chain of goalie schools. He was later able to sell his services as a coach to multiple teams through a combination of video instruction and bi-annual on-site visits. He also started a firm specializing in building closets.

When his Fife Flyers made eight-hour bus treks to and from the London, England, area for games, Briere put the travel time to good use and founded a bio-tech company. "That was even though I knew shit about bio-tech," he admitted. "I'd failed chemistry."

What he did have was a five-point business plan for finance, research, and marketing that he was later able to apply to help build confidence in the game's most demanding position. "Even if you know nothing about goaltending," he said, "there are elements you can [identify]. We all know a confident goaltender is better than a good goaltender any day."

That mind-set starts with not treating goalies as outsiders at practice. "Head coaches hate the dead angle goal," Briere said. "They say, 'How did that go in? That's a real team killer.' So I ask the coaches, 'When was the last practice with dead angle shots on the goalie?' Goalies will say 90 percent of the game is mental. So I ask them, 'When did they work on that part?' Goalies only start working on the mental side when they start struggling. By then it's too late."

In Briere's quest for superior professional development to pass on to students, he visited Finland, the world's goalie factory, where the position is exalted. He also took in training sessions at the U.S. Navy Seals headquarters in San Diego. He noted that positive reinforcement for recruits trumped what he thought would be Hollywood scenes of constant yelling and intimidation like in films such as *An Officer and a Gentleman*. "The instructors would say, 'Great job, but it would be even better if you did this or that,'" Briere recalled of their teaching methods. "So praise the goalie every day, and then when they achieve something, that's when you can raise the bar a bit. Being a goalie was the greatest gift I was given. It's not like the old days when you had no [mask] and were getting hurt all the time. All the things a goalie can do now, being a leader, seeking to be better, facing adversity at a young age... you're going to have that [benefit] the rest of your lives."

CHAPTER 13
THE WILD WEST

"Only in the West." That was the quip that started or ended innumerable time zone tales involving the Leafs, who had a knack for making news when most of Toronto had gone to sleep. The arrival of the Los Angeles Kings, Oakland Seals, Vancouver Canucks, and a bit later, the Edmonton Oilers and Calgary Flames, seemed to throw everyone's behavioural body clocks off, and that meant plenty of entertaining yarns.

If there was a team discipline issue for the Leafs or a dust-up with the law, it always seemed to occur at night in those destinations. That was also the case for big trades, player MIAs, and unscripted events with a coach or front office member. Western trips also seem to coincide with increased chances of overtime, a major injury, or a late-breaking team or individual record set in either triumph or futility. That made it exciting for fans and players, but not so much if your job was defined by Eastern print deadlines.

One of the first Western episodes for the Leafs was when Hall of Fame goalie Jacques Plante languished too long in the California sun. Teammate Ron Ellis said his head looked like a ripe tomato, and he was unable to put his mask on by game time at the "Fabulous" Forum. Young Bernie Parent—yet to be traded to the Philadelphia Flyers—had to start. The Leafs record in those two Calfornia cities was 4–8 before they finally swept a trip.

In John Brophy's tenure as coach, Toronto did not win a game in L.A. And the volatile coach departed the Forum one night with a painful souvenir. Banging his head on a metal girder beneath the stands, blood came spurting right through his famous white mane while he stoically stayed on the bench. "He didn't even want the trainers to help him," Mark Osborne said. "He just kept saying, 'Bleed, bleed.' With that big red spot and his white head, he looked like the Japanese flag."

One of my first trips to the West was in February of 1989, where a struggling Leafs team pulled into L.A. Brophy had been fired two months earlier, and an initial rally under George Armstrong had faded. There had been no team captain the previous three seasons since Rick Vaive was deposed. In such a leadership vacuum, it was hardly a shock that some young Leafs went astray. Forward Ken Yaremchuk was apparently over-served after a 5–4 loss, and police were called to deal with a man on a busy thoroughfare pretending to be a bull-fighting matador. He was using his suit jacket as a cape to challenge oncoming cars. When Leafs personnel went to the station to reclaim Yaremchuk, amused officers informed them he'd tried to arrange his own release, loudly insisting, "Don't you know who I am?"

A stern assistant coach, Garry Lariviere, met Yaremchuk at the airport the next morning, separated him from the team flight, and sent him home on suspension. Toronto went on to its next stop in Calgary, where the Yaremchuk affair was naturally big news. Forward John Kordic was one of the first off the bus at the Saddledome. He raced to a rink entrance with iron security bars on the window and began shaking them, as each Leafs player passed, while shouting, "Don't you know who I am? I'm Ken Yaremchuk!"

* * *

Maple Leafs left winger Bill Berg slams the Los Angeles Kings' Luc Robitaille into the boards during the teams' contentious playoff series in 1993.

The Leafs–Kings' 1993 conference final playoff was a saga unto itself. The series moved west after an acrimonious split in Toronto. The Kings won by a goal in Game 2. There were echoes of a rousing Game 1 fight between Wendel Clark and Marty McSorley after Clark came to the aid of Gilmour after McSorley flattened him in that first game. "No one had ever taken a run at Gilmour before," Clark wrote later in *Bleeding Blue*, "and it looked like McSorley was aiming directly for his head. I saw red and I knew I had to answer the bell and stick up for our best player. This wasn't a strategic fight. My blood was pounding. McSorley and I stood there, raining rights down on each other's heads. I didn't position him or circle around him. I was just pumping my fist back and forth as fast as I could. Marty had used the hit to tell us the Kings were coming after each and every one of us—even our skilled players. At moments like this, rivalries are built."

Even the coaches were getting into it. Pat Burns objected to what he saw as overt rough-and-tumble tactics by opposite number Barry Melrose. At one point at the Gardens, Burns lost it, barging across the thin line of spectators that separated the two benches at the time. Burns had to be restrained by Leafs doctors stationed in No Man's Land. As Burns kept threatening him, Melrose puffed out his cheeks and stomach and strutted up and down the bench to mock the Leafs coach's girth. "I thought he was ordering a hot dog from the vendor behind me," Melrose joked.

A cousin of Clark's and a one-time thumper in the employ of the Leafs, Melrose could handle himself. However, knowing how former cop Burns loved a street fight, Cliff Fletcher said, "Let's just say Barry was a lucky man that night that Pat didn't reach him."

Melrose had also raised the ire of *Hockey Night in Canada*'s Don Cherry, who needed no urging to back his beloved buds so close to a Cup. When Melrose refused to let the Kings do any pregame interviews because he didn't like Cherry kissing Doug Gilmour after an earlier playoff game, Cherry turned his guns on the Kings' coach, starting with his mullet. Kings fans were already complaining that the *Hockey Night* announcers were cheerleading for a Toronto-Montreal final. Ironically, many in Canada were convinced commissioner Gary Bettman was going to influence an L.A. win to salvage American TV ratings in the championship.

When the Leafs arrived for Games 3 and 4 at their swank oceanfront hotel, the Loews Santa Monica, a local sports show host sent dozens of donuts up to Burns' room. It was a prank to mock the weight of Burns, a former policeman who supposedly could not refuse donuts. The host was advocating Kings fan deliver more to the Leafs bench during the game. But Burns and his assistant coaches turned the tables by taking the boxes of beignets down to the beach and kindly distributing them to the homeless.

Between Games 4 and 5 and with the series split, the Kings came back to Toronto on millionaire owner Bruce McNall's private jet. Melrose went back to the past—way back—for a inspirational sports analogy. "When [the Spanish explorer Hernan] Cortez landed in North America, he burned the three ships, and his soldiers marched," Melrose said. "There's no going back to Spain. The soldiers had to fight to get across the country. That's motivation."

Reporters asked how Melrose would get this same message across to modern-day players asked reporters. "I'm going to burn the plane when they get to Toronto," Melrose said laughing.

Game 6 at the Forum was a chance for the Leafs to end the series and earn some rest for the next round. It became one of the most controversial finishes to a game in Toronto playoff history. The completion of a Clark hat trick had put the Leafs on the right path, giving them a lead after shoddy penalty kept the Kings up early in the game.

Then came the fateful missed call by referee Kerry Fraser on a Wayne Gretzky high stick that struck Gilmour in the face. Under rules of the day, it should've been considered game misconduct, but Gretzky stayed in the game and scored the overtime goal. Still vilified by many fans in Toronto, Fraser tried numerous times to explain what happened that night: "As the Kings set up on the power play, I was down by the far circle, away from the puck," he reflected in The Players' Tribune. "Gretzky gets the puck, shoots it, and my eyes go to the net. But Jamie Macoun blocks it. The puck rebounds between Gretzky and Gilmour. When my eyes go back to Gretzky, I see a motion. Gilmour goes down. Did Gretzky's stick catch him? Gilmour's bent over. He's got blood on his chin. And I have no idea what happened. That's a helpless, helpless feeling. It was a huge call to make, a worse one to miss."

If Gretzky had hit him on the follow-through of a shot rather than used his stick recklessly, Fraser would have had some leeway. "Guys from both teams were skating up to me," he wrote. "It didn't smell right. I should have known when I saw Gretzky skating away. Whenever there was a dispute, Gretz was always at the forefront, arguing his side of it. But this time he kind of slinked away. That was uncharacteristic. That should have tipped me off. But to be honest, I was attempting to roll back the play in my mind over and over, looking for some measure of recall that would provide the evidence I needed. I'm starting to think, *Did I miss this?* I skated to my linesmen and said, 'Guys, help me out.'"

Ron Finn had the balls of an elephant and said, "Kerry, I didn't see it. I was looking through their backs."

Kevin Collins, who had conducted the end zone faceoff, said, "Well...I dunno. In referee school they hammer it into you: call what you see. Don't guess. The honest to God truth is: I didn't see it. I had to eat it. I said, 'No penalty.'"

Leafs brass at the game were incensed. What other conclusion for the blood on Gilmour's chin could there have been other than a high stick? "Did the puck shoot up through a hole in the ice and hit Doug?" Assistant general manager Bill Watters raged.

More than a quarter century later, the Leafs have never been that close to a cup, and Gilmour is still peeved. But he cut (pardon the pun) Fraser some slack that the replay technology and two-referee system that would've backed Toronto's case was not around in '93. "It wasn't until the next day that I saw another angle of the play on television," Fraser said. "You could clearly see Gretzky high-sticking Gilmour."

Threats and crank calls dogged Fraser and his family for days after the series. At the home of Fraser's parents in Sarnia, Ontario, an irate Leafs fan drove 160 kilometres from Kitchener to ram the family camper in the driveway until Fraser's father chased him away with an axe. For a while Fraser's mother kept a referee's whistle near her bed in case she had to signal for help. "At the time, I had no idea the call would follow me for the rest of my life," Fraser said in another interview with the *Toronto Sun*. "I have a hard time forgiving myself when I look at the replay that is constantly being shown by you guys. Nonetheless, we are human. That was human error and one that unfortunately had some consequences."

Everyone knows what happened in the deciding match. Gretzky played what he called "the game of my life" and staked his team to a big lead and recorded a hat trick in an eventual 5–4 win. But No. 99 also had pregame motivation: the criticism that followed the high stick and the commentary from some quarters that he was no longer his dominant self and that Gilmour was outplaying him. And just before Game 7, there was a fateful chat with a security guard at the Kings' Toronto hotel. The ever-gregarious Gretzky inquired how the guard's day was going and was told it was quiet at that point. He told him to just wait until around 10:30 PM, when a downtown party would surely ensue after the Leafs won. Gretzky smiled and told the guy not to worry about late-night celebrations "because my job starts at 7:30."

Before the Game 7, Toronto comedic actor John Candy, a business partner of McNall, was given permission to say a few words. "It was right around the time, normally, when Barry would speak," winger Mike Donnelly told the *Los Angeles Times*. "He said, 'Well boys, you know what's at stake.' He was kind of serious. We just started laughing. I think he just made us all relax a little bit more. You're going into an elimination game. You've got the best player in the world on your team."

*   *   *

Before the NHL brought in its shootout tie-breaker rule in 2005, the possibility of the 0–0 game was always there, though it was less so in the 1980s because goaltenders or their smaller equipment just weren't as good as today. I was "lucky" enough to cover a nil-nil game—possibly the last ever in Leafs history if the current shootout rule is kept. This double-knot had drama to it and, of course, it was on Pacific time.

The Leafs were in San Jose for the first of back-to-back road games. Coach Mike Murphy preferred Felix Potvin play in Calgary the next night, so he flew ahead to be well-rested. Glenn Healy started, and the Leafs called up Marcel Cousineau from St. John's, all the way across the continent, as a backup. With 4:01 to play in the scoreless match and a puck loose near the Toronto crease, Healy lunged with his catching mitt to cover up. But Sharks forward Bernie Nicholls stepped on his exposed hand, causing a deep cut. The ice-cold, jet-lagged Cousineau was summoned to make the remaining regulation and overtime stops. He and Healy combined for 22 saves and the first 0–0 Toronto road game in 40 years. "I feel very fortunate the injury wasn't worse," said Healy, who needed eight stitches right down to the tendons on his right hand. "He was trying to kick my hand to get the puck loose."

"Nicholls went in there to get a puck that was well frozen," an angry Murphy said. "You naturally take exception to that."

Cousineau, who had coincidentally combined in a shutout win with Potvin in one of his previous Leafs appearances during his rookie year of 1995–96, kept adding to his frequent flyer miles by coming along to Calgary. "You never expect to go into a 0–0 game," Cousineau said. "I was in a bit of shock on the bench…I just didn't want to let in that one goal."

* * *

The Flames and Oilers also had something of a curse going where the Leafs were concerned, though the latter usually involved Gretzky tearing up Toronto's ranks in Northlands Coliseum. He always saved something extra for the Leafs, knowing family was watching back in Brantford, Ontario. Alberta was where Leafs winger Mike Gartner suffered a punctured lung in a game against the Oilers on February 3, 1995. It was deemed too dangerous for him to fly on to Calgary and then Toronto, so he had to take a few days' rest and come back east by way of cross-country train.

Two former Oilers left the Leafs in the midst of Western trips. Goalie Grant Fuhr failed to show for a 1991 flight from Winnipeg and did not contact the team for almost 24 hours.

It turned out the one-time member of Edmonton's Stanley Cup dynasty was having worse adjustment problems than anyone thought after being traded to the sad sack Leafs. Family matters were complicating his life at the time, but he and Fletcher talked it out, and Fuhr eventually became part of a Leaf ressurgence the following season.

A few years earlier, enforcer Dave Semenko left the team entirely. Though he should have been a kindred spirit with Brophy, the aging former bodyguard for Gretzky detested the latter's coaching style. When Brophy ripped into Semenko in front of other Leafs for drinking wine during an in-flight meal, a minor violation of team policy, the enforcer had enough. The plane landed in Vancouver, but Semenko boarded another for Edmonton and never played again.

Six years after he was traded in a rebuild, Gilmour was picked up by the Leafs in the late stages of the 2002–03 season. The intent was one last hurrah in blue and white when playoff time arrived. On his second shift of his first game in Calgary, where Gilmour had joined the Leafs from more than a decade earlier, there was a mid-ice collision with Dave Lowry, and the two locked legs. It was the last NHL game the 39-year-old Gilmour played.

* * *

Vancouver, usually the last stop for the Leafs on their Canadian trips, featured its share of twists. Before 2018–19 there had been a total of six overtime games in regular season and playoffs at the Rogers

Centre and PNE Coliseum. On New Year's Eve 2002, the Leafs were in Vancouver and down to 16 men at one point. Already missing injured top liners Sundin, Alexander Mogilny, and Mikael Renberg, they started the festive evening one man below the game limit. During the match they lost Nik Antropov and Ric Jackman to injuries and Tie Domi to a misconduct. But on the stroke of midnight in the East, Jyrki Lumme fired the winning goal.

In one of a couple of Vancouver road games played less than two months apart in early 2000, Toronto blew a four-goal lead with 15 minutes to play, including a Markus Naslund short-handed goal with 40.8 seconds to go in regulation. But Sundin, floored by a Matt Cooke major for kneeing earlier in that game, returned in time to score on Garth Snow. "We thought it was a picnic out there," a livid Pat Quinn said. "We should have had a blanket set out and had tea and crumpets. It was a joke."

Running some questionable interference for Sundin's goal was linemate Steve Thomas who had scored in overtime with five seconds to play after the Leafs let a 4–1 lead get away in their previous Vancouver visit.

* * *

In mid-January of 2008, the perfect media storm ensued in California in the last days of John Ferguson Jr.'s tenure as general manager. Near the bottom of the conference and winning just one game after Christmas—by shootout—the Leafs winged their way west to play Anaheim, L.A., and San Jose after losing to Pittsburgh and Philadelphia. It was becoming evident they'd miss the playoffs a second time under head coach Paul Maurice, which put his future in doubt. Then there was captain Sundin and the question of whether he'd stay in blue and white beyond that season. The soap opera about him playing out his time in Toronto without dropping his no-trade clause was nearing its climax. Also on the trip were Ferguson and assistants Mike Penny and Jeff Jackson, who'd came for scouting meetings held simultaneously with the trip.

A bigger distraction was the presence of Richard Peddie, the CEO of Maple Leaf Sports and Entertainment (MLSE), who claimed he was hitching a ride to see L.A. Live, the development around the new Staples Center, to borrow some ideas for new Maple Leaf Square at the Air Canada Centre. But many thought he was there to see for himself how fractured the team had become. He'd already admitted it was a mistake to hire the inexperienced Ferguson in the first place. The swing started with a 5–0 thrashing in Anaheim. The Leafs were overwhelmed by the Mighty Ducks, the defending Cup champions. "It's discouraging," Maurice said. "We have to find a way to get these guys going."

On the next night against the Kings, who were then cellar dwellers on their side of the conference, results were just as bad. Andrew Raycroft, the goalie Ferguson put so much faith in before trading for Vesa Toskala, let in four first-period goals, and Toronto fell 5–2. Fergie bolted the press box after two periods, putting in a call for yet another stopper, farmhand Justin Pogge, whom Ferguson had pegged as goalie of the future to justify his trading of Tuukka Rask.

On the next day, practice was canceled for a late-afternoon team meeting in the lobby of the Leafs' hotel, after which the travelling press was given a few minutes of access before the club boarded a bus for a flight to San Jose. It evolved into one of the craziest days ever on the beat.

Before the players awoke, more trouble was brewing back in Toronto. Opinionated analyst Glenn Healy was on radio, claiming sources told him half the team had already quit on Maurice and the other half "didn't care." Then came a tip to the *Toronto Sun* that the Leafs had postponed a scheduled team photo for the following week, a signal that one or two players or club personnel would not be around much longer. The MLSE board was scheduled to meet at some point in January to re-assess Ferguson's fate, and there was speculation that he could be fired as early as that day via a conference call with Peddie.

The NHL chose that moment to announce its full All-Star game roster with Sundin the lone Leafs rep in Atlanta later that month. Sundin quickly announced he'd decline to go, a highly unusual move for the proud Swede, which fuelled rumors that he was about to leave. That created a wild scene of four different big-ticket scrums: Maurice, Sundin, Ferguson, and Peddie.

Emotions ran high, especially for the normally composed Maurice, who used his platform to take a swipe at Healy. Ferguson, who was feeling let down by several significant contracts such as Jason Blake and Darcy Tucker, didn't sugarcoat the big picture. "To hear that anyone is not disappointed with the effort recently would be surprising," he said. "I'm responsible for everything that goes on here."

Peddie was among the last to board the bus and had to answer for a situation many in Leafs Nation had come to loathe: a coddled team in a high-end market was treated like gold in a sold-out building but not re-paying that faith on the ice. "I've seen all the clippings from the Toronto papers today and I'm seeing a lot of fans who paid to come out to two or three of the games here," Peddie said. "I feel their angst. We're all disappointed."

The bus pulled away, leaving four story angles—all worth a front page on their own on any other day—with the clock ticking toward 8:00 PM and deadlines back east. Most of us had checked out of hotels that morning but raced back with our luggage and convinced the manager to let us camp out at the business centre. We crammed an eventful day into about 90 minutes of writing time, while reporter and designated driver Dave Shoalts channeled his inner Andretti to roar through America's worst rush hour traffic to the airport and return our rental car. We barely made the plane and a night cap in San Jose. Seldom has a beer tasted so good after a work day.

The Sharks edged the Leafs 3–2, and, though Toronto staged a mini-rally to win the next three games, Ferguson was fired after a loss in New Jersey on January 22.

CHAPTER 14
COACH'S CORNER

One of the greatest Maple Leafs coaches got into the profession because—of all things—a skateboard accident. Kalli Quinn watched her father, Pat, suffer the injury that ended his playing career as one of the NHL's most physical defenceman. It didn't happen on the ice. It happened on the driveway of their Atlanta home. Pat was fooling around with skateboards he bought for Kalli and sister Val. "We had a steep driveway. He went to jump off the board because we had a car parked at the bottom," Kalli recalled the day she accepted Quinn's Hockey Hall of Fame ring in 2016. "He just landed the wrong way and snapped both bones in his ankle. He tried to play the next year, and it wasn't great."

Through on the ice at age 34, Quinn eventually turned to coaching. "He accepted [the skateboard mishap] because if it didn't happen that way, he wouldn't have had the opportunities he had afterward," Kalli said.

No Leafs figure since Conn Smythe knew more military history than Quinn. His father, John Ernest Quinn, served aboard Canadian destroyer escorts in World War II on convoy duty during the Battle of the Atlantic. He attained the rank of petty officer while dueling the German U-boats. "He would talk about the 60-foot seas buckling the front of some ships, but there were things he saw that he didn't want to speak about," Quinn said.

Quinn's grandfather, George "Snooze" Ireland, was a munitions carrier in the Canadian army in World War I before a football career in Hamilton. On Remembrance Day, Quinn would take to heart the words of John MaCrae's famous poem, "In Flanders Fields." "It's such a powerful verse," Quinn said. "And it became part of the motto of the Canadiens' dressing room."

As coach, Quinn would try and make his players aware of that sacrifice but also work in a military theme to his pregame speeches. "Quinn was one of the best orators ever," declared Glenn Healy, who was quite the history student himself. "He would get a chair, put it in the middle of the room, and tell stories about the war and how it would be similar to the ice. One day he got into something called the British box-plus-one, how it had led to a great victory, and we were going use the same strategy. He went through all the logistics of how it had worked for them and how it was going to work for us. I can't remember what war he was talking about. I just thought it was a great story, a great speech, and we were all buying in. But I think Pat failed to realize we had about five Russians on the team. The question from all of them afterward was, 'Hey Glennie, what the hell is the box-plus-one?' Pat was the funny sort. He would take the black marker and write a lot on the whiteboard, then wipe it off with his hand. Then he'd [get animated] and start touching his face so he'd have the marker all over it. We didn't want to say anything, but the whole room would be trying not to laugh. [Assistant coach] Rick Ley would kind of give him a hand signal to rub it off. But we really did have a good group of guys. There were probably nine of them that could have been a captain, such as Gary Roberts. But Mats could speak with a pretty strong voice. It's just too bad we didn't win. We were right there for three of those years."

Although other Leafs coaches certainly smoked, they kept the habit well out of the public eye, especially after health warnings began in earnest during the 1970s. Not Quinn, who loved a good cigar and was always seen coming and going from the rink with one in his mouth, hand, or breast pocket. His wide popularity meant he could flaunt many of Toronto's tough smoking bylaws. Because Quinn was the first coach to set up office at the Air Canada Centre, it took the building staff a couple of tries to get the ventilation right when he lit up. In the first few weeks, the fumes were somehow going right into the Raptors' dressing room. "In New York they always knew when the Leafs were in town," equipment man Brian Papineau said of the tight corridors before Madison Square Garden was renovated, "because Pat's cigar smoke would be coming down the hallway before us."

The back door of the Leafs' room at the Air Canada Centre doubled as the gym door, and fitness buff Gary Roberts could often be found leading some team exercises. But he was often undermined by Quinn and his stogies. "The door would fly open, and in would come Pat with a big Churchill cigar lit up about 20 feet long," said equipment man Scott McKay. "Pat didn't give a shit that it was 8:30 in the morning, and the smoke was wafting through the room."

The irony was the Air Canada Centre's in-house announcement that it was a smoke-free facility. "In Boston a security guy comes to our door at about 5:30 on a game night, wearing a uniform and asking for a team official," McKay said. "He said very sternly, 'Somebody on your team is smoking. Can I see them?' There was no way to hide who it was, so I took the guy in and knocked on Pat's door. He and Ley had big cigars, and I said, 'I think there's a fireman out here.' Pat said, 'Send him in.' He listened to the guy tell him it was a no-smoking building and all that, then Pat says, 'Get the hell out of here, you goddamn tree hugger. This is our room. You don't tell us what to do.' He always protected his team and his staff, a great guy to work for."

The only thing that gave Quinn more pleasure than cigars was sniping at officials. This went back to the 1980 Stanley Cup Final when Quinn's Philadelphia Flyers lost Game 6 to the New York Islanders when two controversial offsides were not called on New York. One was after the overtime Cup winner by Bob Nystrom. Had video review been around, it would've likely backed the Flyers, even though there was no guarantee they would've won a Game 7. Anyway, 20 years later, it was still bugging Quinn, who badgered the zebras often. The Leafs bench often got caught up in the emotions and became known for a time as the most unsportsmanlike outfit in the NHL. "We were in Boston one night," McKay said. "The referees walk by our room, and Pat calls one of them 'Yellow,' going old-school with his insult. All that stuff is pretty funny. There was an NHL referee from my hometown, Kincardine, Ontario—Kevin Pollock. But instead of chatting with me if he came by our bench, it was just a wink because we both knew if Pat ever caught you talking to the refs, he'd be all over you. I always had to be careful. One night in Toronto, I'm at the end of the bench, and Pat starts screaming, 'Scotty, get down here!' I run to the middle of the bench, ducking low, so I'm not blocking the view of people in their $5,000 seats, and say 'What's wrong, Pat?

He says, 'Son, take my jacket. There's a rip in my pocket, and my glasses have fallen into the lining, and I can't get them."

It made quite a scene. Quinn was straining to see the action with poor eyesight, and McKay was beside him wrestling with the inner workings of the jacket. "Pat used to wear really nice suits," McKay said. "So I ended up taking it in the room and using a scalpel to get the lining out, so he could see. That was a bit of pressure on me there."

Before coming to the Leafs, Quinn coached Team Canada at the world championships in Moscow in 1986 after his Vancouver Canucks were eliminated from the NHL playoffs. During an exhibition game in Stockholm, Mike Bullard (another future Leafs player) spun in the Canadian zone and slapped the puck to clear the zone. It went directly into his bench and smacked into Quinn's mouth. Quinn was going to need major dental repairs, but the team was already leaving for Helsinki and then on to three weeks in Moscow, where he was wary of having such a procedure done. So Quinn's big appetite and his love of cigars had to be put on hold.

Years later, with the Leafs in Detroit for an exhibition game against the Red Wings, Quinn was struck by a puck again. This headshot was also friendly fire, according to McKay. "And the next game Pat took another one," McKay said. "[Rick] Ley got a helmet and mask from one of our goalies and put it on Pat's desk before practice next day. Pat got a good chuckle out of that. He was pretty serious when the game was on, pretty lighthearted when it wasn't."

Winger Derek King, now a head coach of the AHL's Rockford IceHogs, credited Quinn with almost overnight attitude adjustment. "It had been a different kind of locker room, some guys were looking for new contracts or trades," King said. "We were a bit dysfunctional, but Pat changed that. Individual stats didn't matter; you could be playing with Sundin one night and way down the next, but guys didn't care. Hats off to Pat and the staff, but it also helped we had Mats, Curtis Joseph in goal, and we could run and gun. We came up short in the playoffs, but that was a solid room and a solid team."

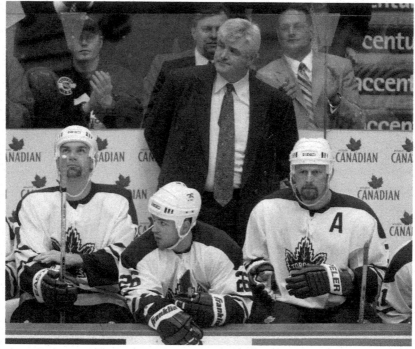

Coach Pat Quinn guides the Maple Leafs during the 2002 Eastern Conference Final.

*   *   *

Usually making his morning media appearance wearing a Leafs ball cap and in sweaty T-shirt (he comes off the ice and goes for a run), Mike Babcock appeared one day in 2017 wearing a University of New Hampshire hockey cap. He was on a streak of losing friendly wagers, and this one was with winger James van Riemsdyk when JVR's younger brother, Brendan, played against Merrimack (Massachusetts) College, where the coach's son Michael attended. UNH won 5–2, and Babcock had to face the cameras in a UNH lid while the Leafs smirked in the background. Babcock lamented he'd had to buy bottles of wine for Auston Matthews, former general manager Lou Lamoriello, and Leafs player evaluation director Jim Paliafito after losing bets based on Canada-U.S. games during the world junior hockey championship.

Babcock's bets fared much better in the 2018 Olympics. The NHL's decision not to participate had been a tough pill for him after being in line to coach Team Canada for the third straight time. He and all the multinational Leafs watched enviously as the tournament unfolded. Naturally, the various players on competing countries started taking flyers on their favourites. First to fall were Leo Komarov and William Nylander, as Finland and Sweden were eliminated. They came to practice and found Canadian National Team sweaters hanging at their stalls, and Babcock was sure to feature them prominently in drills so photographers could catch them in red and white amidst all the blue. "Looked good on me, eh?" Komarov, being a good sport, said afterward.

Nylander, whose Swedes were upset by Germany, had already lost a junior gold bet to Babcock. He was forced to wear an even louder Canadian sweater with a red base and white trim that Toronto assistant coach Andrew Brewer saved from the Sochi games in 2014 when he was on Babcock's staff. It came covered with Canadian player autographs to add to Nylander's discomfort. "You have to hold up your end of the bargain," Nylander said before sighing. Had Babcock lost, he would've had to wear a garish blue and gold Swedish coach's track suit to run the workout.

In 2015 Ancestry.ca gave both Babcock and Dave Keon a jolt by publishing research that they were related. It required digging deep to find that the two are eighth cousins once removed. That connection traced back to a man named Louis Houde, who came to New France, Quebec, in 1647. Both were born in northern Canada—Keon in Noranda, Quebec, and Babcock in Manitouwadge, Ontario, above Lake Superior. Keon came from mining country, and by chance Babcock's dad was a mining engineer from New Liskeard, "I had no idea," Babcock said of their family ties. "I know who Keon is obviously. But an eighth cousin? I have lots of people in Saskatchewan who tell me they're my cousins. I don't think they are but whatever."

* * *

Pat Burns was known as a players' coach, but some Leafs tested his patience. One forward was easily distracted when not on the ice, and when Burns called his name on a line change during a road game in Calgary, he saw the guy was busy watching Flames mascot Harvey the Hound cavort with fans behind the glass nearby. An enraged Burns nearly knocked over several Leafs as he squeezed his large frame down the bench and screamed in the guy's ear to get the hell out on the ice.

Harvey wasn't the first mascot to annoy a coach in Cowtown. Everyone remembers Craig MacTavish of the Edmonton Oilers ripping out Harvey's fake felt tongue when he leaned too far over the boards, and while with the Vancouver Canucks before Toronto, Quinn wanted a piece of him, too. Quinn was near an open gate of the Saddledome during intermission when he saw Harvey's act included wiping his bottom with a Canucks sweater—much to the delight of the fans. That crossed the line to desecration in the eyes of the proud Quinn, who decided he'd personally give Harvey the heave-ho. The mascot spotted Quinn coming his way and likely saw his life in dog years and human flash before his eyes. "But I got about two or three steps onto the ice in my dress shoes, slipping and sliding around, and thought, 'What am I doing out here?'" Quinn said. Harvey was spared.

Though not supportive of opposing mascots, Burns was very supportive of his players. His method of getting his message across usually involved a few minutes of private time—"a beer and a fart"—and things were good. But he wasn't afraid to take shots at players in the media as a means to motivate them; it was usually something biting and memorable. He'd get in the last word that left the player no way to top him. However, he had his limits, too. When he became tired of covering for their mistakes, he would tell the media, "Go ask them what's wrong," and the room would be opened to reveal every Leafs player sitting at his stall with orders not to leave in the half hour allotted for interview time until all reporters had their needed access.

The Leafs wanted to make the biggest public splash possible after landing Burns in 1992.

"We had just got the Montreal Canadiens' coach, a real [coup]," Bob Stellick said. "We decided to introduce him and our new sweaters with the vintage Leaf on the shoulders at an open house at the Gardens. It all came together really quickly. We didn't really have a proper stage for this kind of event, so we set up the Gardens' wrestling ring in its usual centre ice position. Bill Cluff, our marketing guy, got Shopsy's restaurant to donate 8,000 hot dogs, and we got as many Häagen-Dazs ice cream bars as we could. We got Canadian Special Olympics involved, too."

More than 9,000 people showed up for the impromptu open house on short notice, a sign people had not forgotten the moribund Leafs. "We had some indoor pyrotechnics, and Pat spoke a bit," Stellick said. "I remember walking out of there thinking, *This is freaking awesome, like the WWE.* People were so appreciative, and that's when you realized we were sitting on something here."

Burns didn't waste any time putting his stamp on the team. On the first day of training camp, he criticized goaltender Grant Fuhr for being fat.

Cliff Fletcher used to say that over the course of time Gilmour and Burns became one and the same person with their outlooks on the game and life in general. At one point, both were riding fancy Harley Davidson motorcycles. Fletcher was asked if either man was contractually forbidden to ride their hog during hockey season. "I definitely put that in one of their contracts," Fletcher said.

*   *   *

After twice getting to the conference finals in 1993 and '94, the shine was definitely off the Leafs. Despite many of the same crew still being around, there wasn't the hunger or the roster as before despite the best efforts of Mike Murphy, one of the departed Burns' excellent staffers then running the team with Mike Kitchen. "Murph was a great assistant, but it was harder on him as a head coach," Stellick said.

With every win so important to the Leafs' slim playoff chances, Murphy once proposed a faster plane be chartered to get the team back from a road game in St. Louis in time to beat the strict curfew at Toronto's airport for landings after midnight. "We might get two or three exemptions for those late arrivals a year, but that was it," Stellick said. "We usually flew on a turbo prop, but Murph insisted we had to have a jet to save an hour and 10 minutes of flying time. It costs us four times as much. So we lose in St. Louis but do land in plenty of time in Toronto. Next morning, there's a buzz around the dressing room. Someone had called The Fan radio station to complain, saying, 'I was at an airport strip club last night, and about six Leafs came in at 12:30 for last call.' He was a real Leaf fan and it bugged him. So much for our good intentions."

* * *

Coach Roger Neilson made an immediate impression on the Leafs with his collection of rudimentary video equipment back in 1977. He first came upon the idea of isolating game action as a scouting tool during his high school teaching years in Peterborough, Ontario. He saw how much students perked up when film and video was substituted during class lectures and began borrowing the camera equipment from the school, as well as getting a few eager pupils to volunteer to film the Petes junior team he coached at the time.

When it came to editing clips by himself, the first VCRs required him to use both his hands and hold a pencil in his mouth to depress the necessary buttons simultaneously. But at his first NHL camp in '77, when he gathered the Leafs in a small room with a TV under the stands at the Gardens to watch his finished product, they all bought in. "It was new but refreshing, and I was all for it," captain Darryl Sittler said. "Roger got us working on faceoff plays and he probably came up with the first [defined chart] of scoring chances. He played the percentages. You could be a good faceoff guy but not necessarily be on the first line. That was the big thing. He made everyone on our team feel important."

Neilson almost missed the start of a road game against the Montreal Canadiens because he was still up in the stands, instructing students from Concordia University where he wanted cameras positioned and what they were to concentrate on filming. Neilsen's big black briefcase with a large Leafs logo splashed across it was part of the Canadian Museum of History's exhibit on the 100th anniversary of the NHL in 2017. "Roger introduced us to proper off-ice conditioning," Sittler said. "But he didn't coach us like we were in the army. Mostly, he made you accountable to be prepared for every night like it was Game 7 of the Stanley Cup Final. Roger made you a better player and a better individual."

One of Neilson's harder converts was goaltender Mike Palmateer. "I can't say those tapes did anything for me," Palmateer said, laughing. "I had my own book on shooters, and that was in my head. All my career was the same routine: get to the rink, get the heat pack on, grab my coffee, my smokes, and the program with the other team's lineup, then go sit on the can with a couple of the other smokers on the team. I'd read the players' names and say, 'Okay, there's this guy and this guy to watch for.' That was my pregame prep. I guess things have changed a little bit."

Palmateer did embrace a couple of Neilson's ideas to take advantage of loopholes in the hockey rule book. Going back to juniors, Neilson would instruct his goalies to leave their sticks across the crease when there was a delayed penalty or if they were being pulled for a sixth attacker. "The NHL stopped us from doing that," Palmateer said. "But I did one better, knelt on my stick, busted it in two, and since I couldn't play with a broken one, I dropped both pieces in the crease when I left. I did that about a dozen times. Roger was easily the best coach I've ever had. He was ahead of his time for sure. He was not really a motivator, but he had your respect. I don't remember good personal stories about him, but I sure remember the bad ones when he left. Everything went in the toilet."

* * *

When aspiring radio man Joe Bowen was on the Sudbury Wolves bus with Randy Carlyle and Dave Farrish in the 1970s, he wondered if the two fun-loving teens and defence partners would ever get jobs beyond hockey—never mind become NHL coaches. But both thrived, and decades later, they were all together again with the Leafs—Carlyle as head coach and Farrish as his assistant. "I rode the bus three years with both of them," Bowen said. "Both Randy and Dave were great players. Dave was a marvelous open-ice hitter, and Randy was a miserable SOB to play against. Maturity is a wonderful thing, but it hadn't arrived at that point. And we had a lot of time to do things on those long bus rides without any TV or video games."

Bowen recalled the most heartbreaking moment for all the Wolves. It was the deciding overtime game of an eight-point series when the Marlies won the 1975 Memorial Cup. "John Anderson took a penalty for Toronto, and I'm not sure if it was Randy, but the Wolves hit the post three times and didn't score," Bowen said. "The puck bounced out, Anderson left the box, and scored on a breakaway against Jim Bedard."

* * *

Coach Tom Watt was one of the most learned men to coach the Leafs, but walking the beat behind the Leafs bench fired up his temper. Before taking over from Doug Carpenter early in the 1990–91 season, he'd spent 15 years with the University of Toronto, as well as stints with the Canadian Olympic team. With the Winnipeg Jets, he was winner of the 1982 Jack Adams Award as coach of the year. Engaged in a battle of wills with star Dale Hawerchuk, Watt is said to have taken his replica Adams Trophy and stuck it in the player's locker as a reminder of who knew best.

Watt also has a deep appreciation for the game and its place in Canadian history. At every turn he has played up the early development of the sport in Toronto, U of T's connection to the Leafs, and the long-held theory that the logo and colours that Smythe first used when his group purchased the franchise in 1927 were both borrowed from the school when Smythe coached there.

Long before the Leafs re-embraced the military in game night tributes, Watt would stop practice every November 11 at 11:00 AM and gather his players for a moment of silence to commemorate Veterans Day. For some Halloween levity, he donned fake Groucho Marx glasses and a moustache to run practice. At season's end he generously invited Leafs staff and beat writers to his favourite Italian restaurant, Angelini's on Jarvis Street, and retold his favourite hockey stories. Watt had wound up inheriting Harold Ballard's ornate fireplace after the Leafs boss passed away during his tenure as coach.

But some modern developments in the NHL puzzled Watt. When the Minnesota North Stars were among the first teams to introduce a full video screen at the Met Center in Bloomington, Watt was incredulous when they started showing instant replays of Minnesota goals, which naturally roused the home crowd. "That's cheerleading," charged Watt after a game, equating it to the rule that the in-house announcer could not try and use his position to badger or intimidate the on-ice officials or the opposition. Watt's strong feelings on the subject didn't wane for a long time. It got to the point that he planned a protest by pulling the Leafs off the ice after a Stars home goal, risking a delay of game penalty. But that night Toronto shut out Minnesota, and the matter was dropped.

Watt's ultra-competitive streak was also evident in his scrum after a 5–3 home loss to the Calgary Flames. "You can't expect any more when the referee is the brother-in-law of the opposing coach," Watt snapped. The neptism allegation was aimed at Terry Gregson, who'd married Flames coach Doug Risebrough's sister six years earlier. The Leafs, who'd fallen behind 5–0 in the game, had not been given a fair shake on blue paint penalties, in Watt's opinion. "It seemed like [Gregson] made the crease bigger so more people could stand in it," Watt said.

Naturally, the league took a dim view of Watt's rant and fined the Leafs and their coach. Watt said later he had no personal beef with

Gregson's work but that the NHL should not have had him handling games involving the Flames. Watt and Risebrough, however, also had some bad blood from earlier with Risebrough overseeing Watt's departure as an assistant coach of Calgary.

In the days before tablets, coaches had to make rough notes on a real paper pad. Watt entrusted a notebook to Murphy before each game to have at the ready but almost never asked for it until one night in the heat of battle, Watt began barking out, "Pad! Pad!" while staring at the action on the ice. Murphy, who was busy at the end of the bench overseeing forward line changes, didn't hear Watt at first. The coach's call came again, and this time it was louder and angrier: "Pad! Pad!"

Murphy clued in, dug around in his jacket, and, thankfully, the pad was still there. He squeezed past the players on the bench and gave it to Watt, who glared at him for taking so long. But Watt then stuffed the pad in his own jacket pocket—and never took it out the rest of the game. Watt, now in his 80s, remains a pro scout with the Leafs. He is usually at the Scotiabank Arena and always has a good game night yarn to tell.

The late John McLellan spent four years behind the Leafs bench and had this sage observation: "Coaching in Toronto is tougher than coaching in any city in the NHL. It's more of a compliment. It's because the fans are more knowledgeable, and the press is more knowledgeable than in an American city. Four years here seems like eight somewhere else. It's not hockey for [just the regular] season. It's hockey 365 days a year."

CHAPTER 15
PLANES, TRAINS, AND AUTOMOBILES

Before he joined the Maples Leafs, Alex Mogilny caused some disruption with the Buffalo Sabres because of a deep-rooted fear of flying. Growing up in the Soviet Union, he didn't travel often for games or vacation, so it was intense culture shock when he defected to a league that had an 80-game schedule with exhibition and playoffs thrown in. Many of those journeys were on bumpy prop planes. The Sabres and agent Don Meehan knew he was struggling with getting on a plane before he came to North America and hoped he'd be able to overcome the phobia on his own.

But returning from one trip to the West Coast, the Sabres had a brief stop in Detroit. A jittery Mogilny couldn't take any more air time that day and refused to get back aboard, conscripting someone to drive him the rest of the way to Buffalo. He missed other flights that season and at least one game, when he tried to get to St. Louis from Buffalo via train.

Rick Vaive, Mogilny's teammate in Buffalo, sought to help. His own flying aversion could not be cured by hypnosis or psychologists, but he'd stuck it out and tried to help Mogilny.

Vaive arranged for both of them to sit in the cockpit with the pilots while on the ground, talking about what the latter's jobs entailed. That helped a bit, but as coach Rick Dudley noted at the time, "There's not a heck of a lot of [Russian]-speaking psychologists in Buffalo, New York."

Another player used to hang out in the cockpit—but for a different reason. In the late 1980s, aspiring pilot Al Secord was often given permission to sit in with the cockpit crew of the charter and take the controls for a few minutes under supervision, of course. The burly winger went on to a post-playing career flying passenger and transport craft.

* * *

Alexander Mogilny, who used to have a fear of flying, celebrates his game-winning goal against the Carolina Hurricanes in 2003.

When the Hartford Whalers were in the league, only a couple of companies flew direct to the Connecticut capital from Toronto. One was Mall Airways with its noisy turbo props and very tight confines. On one trip Joe Bowen and *Toronto Sun* writer Jim O'Leary were the only passengers on a six-seater. Bowen had scored a bottle of Baileys Irish Cream at the duty-free shop because the mall atop the Hartford Civic Centre was usually shut tight after games, and good bars were a fair hike away.

And it was Bowen who happened to look out not long after takeoff and see heavy smoke billowing out of one of the two small engines. As the pilots were right in front of them but not noticing anything amiss, Bowen leaned forward and advised them to check the wing. "One of them blurts out, 'holy shit!' which wasn't exactly reassuring," Bowen said.

The crew was able to get the trouble under control, but it meant shutting the engine down and making plans for an emergency landing in Albany, New York. The pilot assured the passengers he could make it there safely with just one engine but advised Bowen and O'Leary to remove all sharp objects from their pockets. The nervous duo did so but also cracked open the Baileys, figuring it might be their last drink.

The plane landed safely in Albany, and that's when Bowen noticed how young the pilots really were, looking fresh out of high school—and now a whiter shade of pale. Bowen asked them if this mishap had ever occurred. "Only on the simulator," said one of the shaken lads.

Steve Thomas recalled another hairy landing on the club's charter service in the early 1980s. "It was Air Ontario, but we called them Air Treetops," Thomas said, chuckling. "Once we were coming into Toronto and came down pretty hard. Borje Salming always sat at the back of the plane right beside one of the exit doors, and when we hit, it flew open. Everyone looked around, and all you could see was Borje with his tie blowing around his head in all that wind."

Harry Neale, who coached in the league and accompanied the Leafs on many a road trip, recalled his scariest flying incident while coaching the Detroit Red Wings. The club's plane took off, seemingly without a hitch, until Neale and others looked back on the runway to see part of one engine still there in a mini fireball. They made it to their destination, "but we lost 7–1," Neale said.

It seemed nothing could save the Leafs on the ice in the 1980s, but a little divine intervention was needed on at least one flight. "One of our charter flights, the engine caught fire," defenceman Fred Boimistruck said. "We heard a bump but didn't know what it was until we were landing and saw all the fire trucks on the runway. That was the year that Laurie Boschman had been in the news [clashing with Harold Ballard about his staunch Christian beliefs], and he was clutching his bible as we landed."

Scott McKay remembered a particularly turbulent trip after a game in Vancouver on New Year's Eve 2002. "We were going to a game in New Jersey and flew through a bad storm. I fell asleep, woke up, and a bunch of guys were almost screaming like babies. Here's a team full of pretty tough customers, but this was pretty scary. People might not remember we're up there sometimes three or four times a week. Sometimes we have to change planes because of mechanical stuff or change airports because of wind and weather. But the game's gotta go on, right?"

* * *

One trick that was popular among the traveling Leafs—before the Internet and charter flight era—was "the mailman routine." While stopping over in various airports, a player would peruse the magazine racks at an airport news store and quietly remove all the free trial subscription order forms from the middle or the back. When alone he'd fill in another player's name to receive anything from *Popular Mechanics* to *Good Housekeeping*, and that Leafs player would be confused when his mailbox was jammed with all kinds of publications he didn't recall ordering.

Other pranks were a regular part of traveling. As a commercial flight was approaching Toronto Pearson International Airport after a long Leafs road trip, the pilot came on with the usual info about weather and gate arrival. He then announced in a cheery voice that defenceman Bob Halkidis operated a limousine service if any person needed a ride home. Halkidis, obviously the victim of a newcomer's hazing ritual, then traipsed down the aisle wearing a driver's cap (actually one borrowed from one of the pilots) and holding pretend business cards, as passengers looked confused, and teammates roared with laughter.

That was a twist on another famous Leafs plane skit, supposedly hatched by the fertile mind of defenceman Carl Brewer. During a long flight in the days when heavy curtains divided two or three classes of fare, he sneaked up front to a washroom with a bag of props. He suddenly appeared before his mates from the first-class section with no shirt, wearing a gaudy flotation device, and hair dripping wet, and declared, "You should see the pool we have up there in first class."

* * *

Bob Stellick recalled one player in the Pat Burns era who gave him many challenges during the course of road trips. "You were never sure what this guy would get up to," Stellick said, laughing. "I got back to our hotel late one night in Tampa Bay, and the old orange message light is flashing from this guy's room to call him, no matter the time. I reached him, and he said 'I've a friend here who has to get back to Toronto. Could you get her on our [commercial] flight tomorrow? I think it's sold out, but can you help her?'"

Stellick agreed, telling the player to have the friend meet him at 7:30 AM in the hotel lobby. She could come with him to the airport, where he sorted tickets and seat assignments, before the team bus arrived 90 minutes later. "I asked our player how will I recognize her? He just said, 'She'll be nothing like anyone you've ever seen before.' So I go to check out the next morning, and suddenly this beautiful woman, who looks like Elizabeth Hurley, comes up and introduces herself. My first thought? *I've got to get her Seat 1A.* At the airport I used our team clout to get her aboard no problem, but then we had 45 minutes to kill until the team bus arrived. There was a place to get coffee, but it was at the other end of the airport. As we walked through, I could sense the whole terminal watching us. We got talking about jobs, and it turned out she was a stripper. Now I went from wanting to be seen with her to wanting to hide her. But you couldn't hide anyone from Pat Burns and his cop instincts. As soon as we took off, Pat comes up to me and asks, 'Did you get that stripper on our flight?' Pat was the best coach I worked for and part of it was that he could read people really well. He had been hanging around with the Hell's Angels in his day. He had an instinct when things were going wrong and he could smell weakness in a person. He didn't see Cliff as a strong guy, so he pushed him on some issues to try and get his way. But he was smart. He never fought with his best players on the Leafs because he knew the media would make a big deal about it. He picked his spots."

Protein Packs a Punch

When Gary Roberts arrived in 2000, opening the Leafs' eyes to the value of protein shakes, it had a detrimental effect on the flight crews working Toronto's charters. "Protein products like that give you bad gas," Scott McKay said. "It would get so bad on the planes and stunk so much that the flight attendants, who were lovely ladies, were opening coffee packets up and dumping them in the aisles to counteract it. Oh, it was terrible after practice or after a game getting on that plane."

CHAPTER 16
THE 21ST CENTURY

Brian Burke, who ran the show for four years between 2008 and 2013, was a man of many contradictory statements. For example, he publicly accused the Toronto media of putting too much pressure on the Leafs by constantly bringing up the glory days of four Stanley Cups in the 1960s as the drought approached 50 years. "These guys weren't even born in 1967," he'd bellow. "How is it their fault?"

A few weeks later he announced the team was going to wear a new 1967-themed third jersey—no doubt increasing Maple Leaf Sports & Entertainment's coffers. But the frustration of the Stanley Cup curse eventually caught up to him, too. "There are 30 teams in the NHL, and we haven't won a Cup in more than 40," he said at a hockey business seminar. "Somehow, we've defeated the math."

When the Leafs defeated the Ottawa Senators on the road in Game 6 of the 2000 playoffs' opening round, it marked their first win against a Canadian team since beating Montreal in the '67 Cup final. Maybe it was a lucky sign that the wristwatch and wedding band of centre Alyn McCauley, which was lost after Game 4 of the series in the same rink, turned up just before game time. Toronto went on to a 4–2 clinching win.

On December 19, 2017, the Leafs staged a special afternoon home game against the Carolina Hurricanes to mark precisely 100 years since their first night of NHL play—a 10–9 loss by the Blueshirts to the host Montreal Wanderers.

This *next century game* went a lot better for the Leafs. It was an 8–1 win. Reg Noble had the first goal for Toronto back in 1917, and James van Riemsdyk's during the romp over the Canes scored the 20,000th goal in franchise history. "They told me that between periods," said van Riemsdyk, who put the Leafs over the top at 10:34 of the first. "Just to have a small piece of that [history] is pretty cool."

* * *

Today, the Leafs' dressing compound is packed with sports fitness and science gadgetry, state-of-the-art video, a kitchen, and an artsy decorated player lounge. It's actually two rooms in one with a separate area to change into civilian clothes and leave without being seen by the public or media. Yet 1967 Stanley Cup winner and Gardens general manager Brian Conacher, who oversaw the renovation of the Carlton Street room in the 1990s, is among those who thought such comforts and isolation made it almost too cozy so that its denizens would want not to leave for the ice. "A lot of good hockey players used that original [Gardens] room with great success and made me wonder if the current players were pampered too much," Conacher mused.

One of the first things newcomers Brendan Shanahan and Mike Babcock brought to the Leafs dressing room was the tradition of the honourary player stall, which both were familiar with from their time with the Detroit Red Wings. An unused kiosk was named for a departed player, Gordie Howe's, and Vladimir Konstantnov's was the most prominent in the Wings' room at Joe Louis Arena. When Howe passed away in 2016, Shanahan reflected on how his parents used Howe as an example to him to become the ideal all-around player. "My generation grew up watching Gretzky, Messier, and Bossy, but Gordie was such a legend and that was exemplified in our household," Shanahan said. "If you were going to play a complete game, you identified with him. He was probably the best power forward in the game before the term was used in hockey for players such as Cam Neely. It was not just being big and mean; it was being the whole package."

Shanahan and Howe both played in eras when the Wings were the most respected franchise in the NHL. "Gordie would pop in the room sometimes unannounced," Shanahan said. "He asked for no special treatment. It was quite remarkable. Here was a man who had a street outside Joe Louis named for him, yet he considered himself a guest."

The Leafs have now given their stalls the nameplates of such players as Dave Keon, George Armstrong, Red Kelly, and Mats Sundin, as well as tagging rookie camp teams in their honour.

At the start of the 2014–15 season, Shanahan was club president but very little had yet changed on the ice. The Leafs had not recovered from a blown Game 7 lead in Boston two years earlier. The lack of true dressing room leadership was still evident despite general manager Dave Nonis' dogged belief that coach Randy Carlyle could still make the mostly veterans of that time a winner.

Starting with a record of 9–5–2, the Leafs felt good about their chances, but then came three straight losses, the worst of which was a lacklustre 6–2 loss to their old nemesis, the Buffalo Sabres. It triggered a week of shambolic events that exposed the seismic fault lines in the team and its dressing room and sent Shanahan into full rebuild mode.

As Buffalo's rink did not have the escape hatches of the Air Canada Centre, in which a player could completely disappear behind closed doors after a game, a reporter sought a comment from the notoriously media-shy Phil Kessel. He was one of the faces of the franchise with captain Dion Phaneuf and, while Phaneuf would at least make the effort, Kessel would go days without being accountable despite having signed an eight-year, $64 million deal and after publicly vowing he would cooperate with the press. "Get away from me," Kessel snapped at the scribe, an act that received plenty of play that evening on *Hockey Night in Canada*. Much of the next practice was devoted to Kessel being hauled out of his hiding place to explain himself. He whined about being forced to talk every day, which wasn't the case, though he still wanted to be considered part of the leadership group. "It's spelled out in training camp and on a day-to-day basis that when called upon you are to be made available— simple as that," an unsympathetic Carlyle said. "That's what we support."

The next game was at home against the Nashville Predators, a brutal 9–2 loss that whipped up more public anger against Kessel and the other high-priced underachieving Leafs. The Kessel and Phaneuf contracts had come to be viewed as albatrosses in tandem with the ineffective play of the latest free agent, David Clarkson.

The booing that drove the Leafs into their room after that seven-goal setback was as vicious as it was loud—mostly from the cheap seats.

(With its corporate clientele, the lower bowl usually emptied fast, win or lose.) The ongoing furor prompted Nonis to give Carlyle a tentative vote of confidence. It put even more pressure on the following home game with the hot Tampa Bay Lightning in town.

That night the Leafs got it right, bumping off the Bolts 5–2. The outcome was settled early enough that the majority of the media mob had left press row for the elevator ride and long walk to the dressing room. The TV broadcast also broke away quickly, so most observers missed what happened before the Leafs departed the ice.

Cody Franson and Leo Komarov were in the centre ice circle, beginning the ritual of a raised stick gesture to the cheering fans for a home win. Before the raised stick gesture, which Toronto copied from teams such as the New York Rangers, the 2003–04 Leafs had a spontaneous group hug at centre ice after each win, and the players jumped around in a circle like a football team before a game. The ritual carried them all the way to 16 consecutive games with at least one point. "I don't know who started it, but it caught on," forward Tom Fitzgerald said. "It began somewhere in the first two or three wins. It reminds me of that football movie, *Remember the Titans*, when they got together and did that 'woo, woo, woo' thing. It's good for us—something else we can [identify] with as a group. It's a team hug with no one standing on the outside watching."

"It means everyone's playing a significant role in our success," winger Darcy Tucker added. "That's half the battle sometimes."

But no one else went to join Franson and Komarov after that win against the Lightning. Eventually, Kessel went to Phaneuf and said something, and the two started waving teammates off the ice. Gord Stellick, taking his seat in the radio booth for his postgame show, noticed what the players did and quickly put two and two together: this was a screw you to the fans, at least the most fickle group of supporters.

For a team accused of lack of leadership and gumption by their public so long, it was actually a bold, if not misguided, move. Phaneuf tried to say the Leafs were working on a new postgame celebration, but his story didn't match other teammates. As Stellick observed, "the network that had signed off without noticing the snub to the fans now was breaking down the [postgame] video like crime footage."

The next practice saw one of the largest media contingents ever to gather at the doors. The room took forever to open, and then few players were willing to talk about what went down the night before. Phaneuf got into an argument with one overly combative radio commentator. "How does this help the hockey club?" The latter demanded, referring to the non-salute. "Why don't you just get it over with and bite a head off a chicken?"

The mini-protest angered Shanahan and Carlyle, but it did fire up the team a bit. In the next month, they lost only one regulation game, and all seemed well.

The winds shifted again, however, with a 4–1 loss to the Carolina Hurricanes, the beginning of a tumble to 2–7–0. Despite Toronto holding a playoff position, Shanahan fired Carlyle and replaced him on an interim basis with assistant Peter Horachek, one of the club president's mandated hires from the summer to shake up the staff.

Horachek was a very likeable sort, who'd pinch hit for Carlyle in a couple of media scrums to give the latter a break. His hiring was a popular one in and outside the room. The new-look Leafs responded in their second game, a 5–2 home win against the Columbus Blue Jackets, which was preceded by a rare State of the Union address from Shanahan to the players. Just as significant, Shanahan went on TV and admonished departed coach Ron Wilson, who'd publicly picked on Kessel. "He was a good coach, but he's not the coach here anymore," Shanahan said, pointing out that Wilson would have strongly objected to any other former Leafs coach publicly chirping Kessel on his watch.

As a gesture of appreciation to Horachek after beating Columbus, the players presented him with the camo jacket, the Canadian military issue battle fatigues awarded to their choice for hardest worker of the game. The jacket was supposed to be passed between players with each victory, but 11 losses later, it was still Horachek's. Instead of using the win over Columbus as a spark, the Leafs went west and lost all four games and were outscored 12–1. While in Los Angeles after practice— before the club hired a team of sports scientists to deal with nutrition— they were gobbling a giant order of In-N-Out burgers.

Horachek's team posted an eventual record of 8–25–5, but he didn't go down without a fight. After a 5–4 loss to the Rangers—amid Kessel going back into near hibernation and Clarkson demoted to healthy scratch—Horachek lost his temper. In what the *Toronto Sun*'s Rob Longley called "the runaway candidate for quote of the year for its honesty, bluntness, and accuracy," Horachek snapped, "The give-a-shit meter has to be higher."

After two periods that night, the Leafs had just 10 scoring chances to 23 by the Rangers. Fed up fans inundated call-in shows with support for Horachek, though not everyone was pleased with his vocabulary. "Family and friends told me to choose my words better," said Horachek, laughing.

But the downward spiral meant the unfortunate coach lost any leverage to apply for the job full time. One NHL team broadcaster gave a sarcastic vote to Carlyle as Coach of the Year to underline the Leafs' fall from playoff status. Shanahan had a much bigger name in mind for the next appointment.

* * *

The Leafs were excitedly looking to the opening of training camp in St. John's, Newfoundland, in 2001, and their community relations team that had been planning for a year to meet the club's loyal fans on the East Coast. All that unravelled with the tragic events of 9/11. The Leafs stood aghast around dressing room TV sets at the Air Canada Centre on the morning of September 11, watching the towers come down.

Many were in tears, while winger Alex Mogilny fretted about his wife, Natalia, and two children, who resided across the river in New Jersey. It turned out Natalia had been out walking the dog and looked across the river to see the whole terrible spectacle. Forward Jeff Farkas had a girlfriend in Manhattan and, though she was safe, he spoke to former teammate Mike Mottau, who came out of Rangers camp at Madison Square Garden as one of the towers was crumbling. He said he felt the ground shake.

One of the most fortunate escapes that day was by ex-Leafs player Rob Cimetta. At the World Trade Center for a training session at Morgan Stanley investment bank, the alarm in his building sounded when the first jet hit the opposite tower. Cimetta and his co-workers had made it down 20 flights from his office on the 61st floor when the second plane struck his tower above. It took 40 minutes for him and his colleagues to finally get out of the shaking structure, passing a few firemen on the way. "I remember seeing a jet engine in the middle of the street 100 yards from the building, and we finally figured out what happened," Cimetta told *The Hockey News*. "Ten minutes later the building starts to come down. We knew all those [workers and first responders] were in there."

Leafs personnel, who were in St. John's, quickly turned their attention to helping with the massive influx of international airline passengers whose planes were grounded all over Eastern Canada by the security alert. At Mile One Stadium, they helped local officials register the displaced internationals and prepare meals for most of the 6,000 passengers from about 30 rerouted planes while converting the rink into a temporary shelter.

When the Leafs did arrive a few days later, they found each section of seating in the rink was dedicated to a particular flight. Some of the passengers were able to fill in the time watching the Leafs practice until the last of the rescheduled flights were announced. Each departure was greeted by a crowd cheer, and the last guests left a few hours before the Leafs hosted the Canadiens in an exhibition game.

In September of 2019, the Leafs are scheduled to return and have a few days of training camp in conjunction with the launch of their ECHL affiliate, the Newfoundland Growlers. The ECHL was a proving ground for many Leafs, including popular goaltender James Reimer.

He was MVP of the South Carolina Stingrays in 2009, three years after the Leafs drafted him. That league's scheduling and travel demands could be so hard that—by the time Reimer got to the AHL with its regular three-games-in-three-nights routine—he considered it a luxury. "There were some instances in Carolina where we had a sleeper bus for these overnight trips and there weren't enough beds for everyone," Reimer said. "The rookies would have to sleep on the floor. Those were some tough times when you look back at it, but it builds character and it makes you a better person and a better player."

Gill's Medical Advice

Winger Jeff O'Neill's time in Toronto coincided with that of giant New England-born defenceman Hal Gill. "Hal was one of my all-time favourite Leafs," O'Neill said. "On the road, we called him the bag chucker. He never liked to go in his room when we arrived the night before a game. He preferred a few beers. So his room key would barely open the door, he'd fire his suitcase in as hard as he could, and go out. I asked him once why he was so interested in the beers. He just said, 'It calms my nerves,' and that's the way he dealt with things. And his medical advice for everything, whether you had a bruised chest or just a cough, would be to drink some scotch. He thought scotch was the cure for everything. I guess he could [hold a lot of alcohol]. He was 6'7" and ripped. I'm 5'9" and fat. I couldn't absorb it that well."

As the number of Leafs from Eastern Europe grew, some decided to make Toronto and Canada their home. Before his tragic death in the 2011 Lokomotiv Yaroslavl team plane crash, Igor Korolev would sing along when "O Canada" was played before games as practice for his citizenship test. The centre also asked the media to quiz him on prime ministers and provincial capitals for the written component of his exam. Korolev's death was particularly hard on teammate Kris King. "A brother, that's what I called Igor," King said. "He told me one day that Korolev translated to *king* in Russian, and that he and I and Derek

King must be brothers. He was a quiet guy but did the dirty work a lot of people didn't see, which was unusual for a Russian at that time."

At one stage in that era, five Russian-speaking Leafs, who were dubbed the "Moscow Circus" by the press, were on the roster. Korolev, Danny Markov, Dmitry Yushkevich, Sergei Berezin, and Alexander Karpovtsev certainly enlivened the room, though the latter was not a Leafs player for very long and sadly also perished with Korolev.

A prankster once altered left winger Garry Valk's nameplate to read "Igor Volkov" after he spent time on a line with Berezin and Korolev. "Korolev helped all of our young guys with their language and cultural issues in those days," said media relations man Pat Park. "He was so easy to work with. And he was a great influence on Nikolai Kulemin's career with Magnitogorsk before Nikolai came over here. Igor came to watch him play here so we would see him around the wives' lounge at the ACC."

Another Leafs player who'd make the jump from the former Soviet Union was hulking Khazak winger Nik Antropov, the club's first-round selection in 1998. Antropov once had 26 points in a single game, in which Kazakhstan defeated Iceland 63–0 in the European D Pool championships, netting 11 goals and 15 assists.

Literally hungry for the NHL—his first request after meeting new agent Don Meehan was to get a proper meal—Antropov was a surprise first rounder who had other NHL teams on the draft floor scratching their heads when he was introduced. But he played more than 500 games for Toronto and topped 800 overall in the NHL. He, too, went through the citizenship process and is now settled in the Toronto area. "They gave you a book without about 300 items," Antropov recalled in 2018 of the citizenship rites. "You didn't have to know all of them, but there were about 45 questions and you could only get about five answers wrong. At the top naming the provinces and the territories, that was easy. But the questions about the fur traders who first came over and the Hudson Bay Company, those were the big challenges for me. 'O Canada,' I'd been hearing it for eight months straight for 82 games. That was the last task. They bring you to a room to sing it. But I saw some guys just open their mouths, and they just couldn't. I've lived here longer than I was in Khazakstan. My kids, this is their home. I want to be fully Canadian, I guess, but I have to learn my English a little better."

Antropov also makes an attempt to vote in elections: municipal, provincial, and federal.

"I understand [most issues] and, if I don't, I ask my buddies," he said. "But I always make sure to ask them why I should vote that way."

Generous Ralph

Jim Ralph and a couple of members of the Leafs broadcast crew were on the road at a nice steakhouse and happened to sit a table or two away from goaltender Jonathan Bernier and defenceman Stephane Robidas. The players finished eating first, exchanged pleasantries with the group, and departed. When the media members asked for their bill, the waiter explained that Robidas had picked up their entire tab, including the tip. Everyone texted their thanks with the mischievous Ralph, adding, "Hey Robie, I had a coffee afterward, so you still owe me four bucks."

In Glenn Healy's four years with the Leafs, the club was in the playoffs three times, including making it to the 1999 conference final. "We had a year-end party at a big steakhouse place downtown," said Healy, who became executive director of the NHL Alumni Association in 2017. "I had an entire Scottish pipe band show up. They came through, right into our private room, and the whole restaurant is going what the hell? Danny Markov decided he was going to do his Russian dance to the pipe music. Domi tried to do the same, and at that point, Danny threw a shot glass and got him in the head. The chase was on, right out into the street, and they're probably still running after each other today."

Markov and Darcy Tucker had a very amusing interaction. Tucker was a very respected Leafs warrior but did have a penchant for going over the edge. In the 2000 playoffs against the New Jersey Devils, he tried to get under Marty Brodeur's skin, saying he might run over the great goalie if he persisted in hacking at him when he came near the crease. Mark Everson, a writer with the *New York Post*, thought little of Tucker's antics, dubbing him Sideshow Bob after the devious character on *The Simpsons*. A few Leafs players liked that reference so much, they piled on with Sideshow Bob references in the dressing room, just to irritate their friend.

Tucker did have a chuckle when Markov suggested to him in broken English that he needed to cut back his dressing room chatter in that Jersey series and reduce his many TV interviews because they tended to rile him too much. "He's always telling me I need a whole bunch of shut-up," Tucker said, laughing.

Tucker and Daniel Alfredsson had a more contentious interaction. Alfredsson is expected to get in the Hall of Fame one day, an honour that will be applauded just about every place, but in the minds of some Leafs fans. In one of the longest grudges ever held by the locals, Alfredsson is still a villain for an uncalled cross-check on Tucker during a Senators playoff game win back in 2002. Never mind the Leafs eventually won that series, Alfredsson got the onion from Leafs Nation every time he touched the puck in Toronto and also at his home rink, which was always packed with travelling Leafs supporters.

Quinn thundered that Alfredsson should have been "suspended for life" after the Tucker hit, but the '04 NHL All-Star Game was time for a truce. Alfredsson, his great rival Sundin, and Toronto's *RoboCop* Gary Roberts were on the same Eastern Conference team, and Coach Quinn played them on the same line at Xcel Energy Center in Minnesota. "I told Daniel we're going to dump the puck in the corner, but he had better watch out because Gary's going to come in and hit him," Sundin teased before the game.

They turned out to be the best trio in the 6–4 win over the West. "A great guy," Roberts said of Alfredsson. "These are days when you realize we're all just hockey players."

The six-point afternoon saw Alfredsson score two, Roberts net a goal and assist, and Sundin bag two helpers. "You have a guy who can score, a guy who goes to the net, and a smart player in Alfredsson," Quinn said. "They were marvelous."

Roberts did have one gripe. After playing much of the 2003–04 season with Sundin and Mikael Renberg when the two Swedes jabbered in their own language, Sundin and Alfredsson did the same. "Again, I'm in the middle of the conversation," he said, "and going, 'What are you guys talking about?'"

Roberts was not so congenial to other opponents more than a decade later when the alumni of the Leafs and Red Wings met at Toronto's BMO Field in an outdoor game prior to the 2017 Heritage Classic. Participants going as far back as the 1970s were in the match. Roberts irked Kris Draper of the Wings with a hard hit into the boards late in the game, and Draper retaliated with a slash, and it looked like the two were ready to go at it before teammates interceded. "It wasn't fake. I can tell you that," the Toronto-born Draper said. "That's what we are and who we are. You have the intensity and the competitiveness."

Loud Noises

Defenceman Ron Hainsey isn't just one of the oldest Leafs these days. He also could be the loudest. In the heat of battle, Babcock encouraged players to be vocal on the bench and on the ice. "The more you talk, the more you execute in the defensive zone," the coach said. "People that are confident, you can hear them all over the rink, yelling for the puck. You can hear Hainsey [up] in the booth. Some guys you never hear. That's why they never have the puck." Hainsey agreed that chatter and communication are vital but kept in mind most teams have a few foreign-born players who sometimes can't or won't express themselves loudly.

The Leafs will never forget the Blizzard at The Big House, when 105,429 braved the elements to set an NHL record for attendance. Amid fears the Winter Classic would be cancelled when a huge storm struck, historic rivals Toronto and Detroit blotted all the snow with a lot of blue and red at the University of Michigan. As the Leafs emerged from the player tunnel, they were greeted by a fan waving a sign: "This Is History." Yet it was dicey trying to skate in the early going. "I'll never forget the first five minutes of the game," said defenceman Jake Gardiner. "Nazem Kadri was skating up the right side of the boards. Usually, when he has the puck, he never really loses it. But I think there was a couple of inches of snow at that point, and suddenly the puck was six feet behind him."

The game not only was completed, but also provided a storybook finish for centre Tyler Bozak. He tied it and won it in overtime, spoiling the day for his future coach Babcock. Bozak has a giant picture of his overtime goal hanging in his offseason home in Denver. "It's the coolest," Bozak said. "Me coming in on the shootout and all the fans in the background, flurries are coming down, too, so their goalie couldn't see the puck. Maybe I got lucky with that. I have another picture of me and Frazer McLaren in our toques, walking around before the game and checking out the ice. You can see our breath in the photo. I probably got the most texts and calls after that goal than in my whole career, maybe more than my first NHL goal. You think of the coverage that game got in the U.S., Canada, and around the world with all the people who could tune in. They took something of my equipment to the Hall of Fame. I hope it's there somewhere.

"There were so many people, but you couldn't make out faces in the crowd, God no. It was crazy. Just to go out there and look around and see how many people. It was freezing, too, so everyone was battling it. My parents said they saw people go for drinks and by the time they came back to the seats the drinks were frozen."

In the Leafs net, Jonathan Bernier had snow blowing in his face much of the afternoon but stretched a winter hat over his mask to cover the air holes. Toronto's equipment men gave him little heat packets to jam down the back of his pants.

* * *

Maple Leafs fans cheer Tyler Bozak's goal against the Detroit Red Wings during the third period of the 2014 Winter Classic at Michigan Stadium.

The arrival of winger Alexei Ponikarovsky as a regular in the Leafs lineup in 2000 created a dilemma for equipment manager Brian Papineau. "Our nameplates [for game sweaters] are 24 inches long, and his name went two inches over that," Papineau said. "So we did the same thing we did for him in the one exhibition game he played: sewed two plates together."

As of the 2000–01 season, Lou Franceschetti (1989–91) had the longest surname in club history at 13 letters, followed by Ponikarovsky, Mike Krushelnyski (1990–94), Eddie Litzenberger (1961–64), and Pete Bellefeuille (1926–27) all with 12. In 2018 the club drafted one of its first hyphenated surnames, Semyon Der-Arguchintsev, totalling 15 letters. Thankfully, the slightly built Muscovite went by the nickname Sam or "SDA" with the OHL Peterborough Petes.

Papineau also had to order engraved nameplates for every Leafs player to be put above their locker at the main Gardens rink and the practice facility. As the number of Leafs in the 1990s and 2000s increased with a high volume of trades, he and his assistants saved the plates and decorated the walls of their office with the unique alumni collection, including some of those players who were in just a game or two.

Ponikarovsky and the late Wade Belak bore a resemblance to captain Sundin in the early 2000s, which led to some cases of mistaken identity on the road. Belak used to kid Sundin he'd accept a few $100 to be his official doppelganger, wear a hoodie and sunglasses while ambling from the rink or hotel to the bus to ease the autograph crowd on No. 13.

* * *

While the veterans and blue chips on the Leafs roster enjoyed a fancy golf outing before training camp in 2010, Tim Brent was still busy on the ice. A roster spot for the self-described "lifelong Leafs fan" was far from secure, and he stayed off the course and at the club's practice facility working out. Such summer diligence paid off with a place on the team for the season opener against Montreal.

He'd stuck to his NHL dream for four years and three teams with just 20 games to show for it until finally getting a spot at forward with Toronto. The centre from nearby Cambridge, Ontario, was able to secure tickets for both his grandmothers at the Air Canada Centre for his first game. They were able to see his first goal as a Leafs player, as he tipped in a Dion Phaneuf point shot during a 3–2 win.

Brent had a very eventful single season in Toronto. Not long after his debut, he took an errant stick near his eye in a game against the Rangers—the day before Halloween. "Just put some bolts in my neck and some green makeup, and I'm set," he joked.

Less than a week later, his shin pad was shattered by the full force of an Alex Ovechkin overtime power play drive at the Air Canada Centre. Brent felt as if he had been hit in the knee by a sledgehammer and then took a peek at the damage after rolling down his sock. "The whole left shin pad was caved in. That's never happened to me or any of my equipment," Brent said. "Everyone knows he has a bomb, and I guess I experienced it firsthand. It's one of the things you have to do in overtime. There were a lot of ice bags, but it's just another bruise, another war story. I thought of maybe going down to their dressing room afterward and having Ovie autograph it for me before they left."

Brent was nominated as Toronto's candidate for the Bill Masterton Trophy that season.

*   *   *

Shawn Thornton had a long memory. When his Anaheim Ducks captured the Cup in 2007 and he was part of Boston's successful run in 2011, the physical winger and Oshawa, Ontario, native didn't forget to tell people he was once Leafs property. Unable to prove himself at the NHL level, he was chosen in the 1997 draft but moved out while still a member of the St. John's Maple Leafs.

He retained nothing but good memories of playing in Newfoundland and the rented house he shared with mates such as current Leafs assistant coach D.J. Smith. During long East Coast winters when snow would completely block the ground floor of the dwelling where many farmhands lived, Thornton said the occupants simply exited out of second-floor windows across packed snow—sometimes over the roofs of buried cars— and slid down the rest of the way.

Thornton said the heavy snow had another unintended benefit. When the group of roommates were watching TV and didn't want to go to the fridge for an ice cold beer, they positioned a couch next to a sliding side door entrance. They'd take a bunch of bottles and stick them into the snow bank that piled against the house and open the window to pull one out.

Thornton's Bruins and the parent Leafs wound up against each other in the 2013 playoffs, though the former found it hard to work up a lather against his former Anaheim Coach Carlyle on the other bench. "Randy gave me my chance. There was never an easy day under him, but if you showed up and worked, you could go about your business," Thornton said. "He was a very intelligent coach. He went through some plays I'd never thought of. We had a different, older team in Anaheim: Scott Niedermayer, Chris Pronger, Teemu Selanne, a lot of older guys. I was 29 and one of the youngest on the team. Those other guys had a lot of control in that room. They kept you motivated. Under Randy you did your job—or you didn't do it anymore."

* * *

Ken Dryden was appointed Leafs president in 1997. Most fans were willing to overlook his ties to the haughty Canadiens, as long as that experience could get the Leafs back on track. Brian Bellemore, an influential member of the board of directors under club chairman Steve Stavro, strongly pushed for him to replace Fletcher.

But Dryden's initial address to the media had too many mentions of the Cup for the public's liking for a team that had teased in the past and was clearly not ready at that time to challenge. Award-winning author of *The Game*, Dryden was certainly respected for his idealist view of the sport's future. It was his good intention to eventually bring a more experienced exec to be his general manager. Former Montreal teammate Bob Gainey was considered for the post.

But that didn't transpire, and Dryden's meticulous methods and unfamiliarity with hiring procedures led to difficult times. He created a crew as diverse as that of the Starship Enterprise for his first season: "associate" GM Mike Smith (a term never heard before in the NHL), Anders Hedberg as player personnel boss (the first Swede to hold such a position), himself as GM, and Bill Watters, an ally of the departed Fletcher, as his assistant.

A year later coach Mike Murphy was twisting in the wind as the Leafs missed the playoffs a second straight year as Dryden dithered on firing him. In other unusual moves, Dryden called a press conference just to announce he hadn't found anyone to be GM. He eventually decided to assume that job on an interim basis. While he did take an active interest in the day-to-day running of the team, it included a critique of how newspapers' headlines could better reflect Leafs game stories and writing lengthy introductions for public-address announcer Andy Frost for pregame ceremonies. He assembled an eager office team to dream up promotions and improve fan morale, which cynics, even in his own front office, dubbed "K.D. and the Sunshine Band." "The hardest part with Ken was he'd never worked a day in his life in an office," said Bob Stellick, who'd decided to leave the organization soon after Dryden's arrival. "I liked Ken, but he really isolated himself. He could've done better, but he was Bellemore's guy, and you had all these factions at the time."

Ottawa

As much as Toronto fans loved making the trip to Bytown, especially in playoffs, a generation of Ottawa supporters grew up detesting the Leafs. A pre-teen Mark Borowiecki was in front of his TV set in Ottawa, wishing he was on the ice in the thick of it. "I lived and breathed that rivalry," said Borowiecki, who indeed grew up to play for the Senators. "Maybe taking a run at Tucker would've been fun back in the day, but unfortunately, I won't get that chance."

Asked if he had a particular Leafs player he wanted to hit, Borowiecki laughed and said: "I'm an equal opportunity body checker."

CHAPTER 17
THE FIGHTERS, ENFORCERS, AND PRANKSTERS

The Maple Leafs of the 1990s had an exemplary attendance record—mostly because they wanted to get to Maple Leaf Gardens ahead of Doug Gilmour. "He was the king of the pranksters," said former equipment man Scott McKay, now a project manager with the NHL Alumni. "You knew some monkey business was going to go on. He'd get dressed early for practice—to this day he still hates being late—and he'd go out to the bench where all the water bottles were located. He'd skate around, go to the boards, and undo about three or four caps just enough so they wouldn't fall off, go around again, do four more until they were all done. As soon as coach Pat Burns called all the boys over for water, they all dunked water over themselves. Dougie knew his limitations with Burnsie [and to] not to include him in those gags very often. But one of his favourite tricks with the coaches was to come in early to the coffee machine where we had styrofoam Gatorade cups. He'd innocently ask for one of our great big sewing needles that we fixed equipment with. He'd poke tiny holes in each one. So players would be drinking, and their coffee would be pouring down the front of their shirts."

McKay pitied little Siberian Nikolai Borschevsky, who took hours to work on his sticks, only to have Gilmour try and sabotage his efforts. "Dougie would let him do his thing, wood flying everywhere, the floor covered with sawdust," McKay said. "Nikky would shave the handle down just right, five or six sticks at a time, and it probably took the poor bugger an hour to do it. One day Dougie gets in there early before practice when he's sanding his sticks, wood planing, doing it all. When Nik went into the lounge, Dougie grabbed a saw and cut them all just enough. First shot, snap, second stick, snap. This went on for all five sticks with Borschevsky swearing in Russian about Doug."

When lumber or composite sticks broke in the heat of battle, McKay, his boss Brian Papineau, and others, such as Bobby Hastings and Tommy Blatchford, have to hustle to fetch replacements. Sometimes they are singled out as the heroes if a big goal is scored with a new twig they supplied. There can also be mistakes where the wrong stick is exchanged, or a lefty is given a right-handed stick. Glenn Healy liked to keep his beat-up sticks around to the point where McKay and co-worker John Van Beek started marking the knobs with a dot, so they would know which ones to keep or toss out. Van Beek collected the discarded ones to donate to kids in the area.

But in one home game, coach Pat Quinn was impatient with a sluggish effort from starter Curtis Joseph and ordered Healy to get ready. McKay handed Healy his stick and realized there was no dot on it. "I just looked at Beeker in panic because that meant we'd tossed all his good sticks that day," McKay said. "We had to figure out a stall tactic so I could run out to his truck in the snow and get Glenn's proper stick. You work on the spur of the moment in those situations, and that's why we always encouraged our guys to put numbers on their sticks. Pappy has been credited with being quick at the buffet table, but he's been here the longest and he's pretty quick getting sticks out there. He's been credited with some assists from the players because of that.

"When we're on the bench, you have to pay attention. If you're at the game or watching on TV, it might look like we're just standing there, but at any time, a guy's gear could break or a goalie's strap, so you have to be prepared for that. But sometimes if there's a break, it's okay to look at pretty women in the crowd."

*   *   *

One day when Tie Domi and the Leafs were playing in Boston, talk at the morning skate came around to all the fine colleges and universities in and around Massachusetts' elite educational hub. McKay recalled Domi piped up that he'd once turned down a hockey and soccer scholarship to a big school outside of Chicago. "Healy decided to call BS on that," McKay said, laughing. "Glenn had played at Western Michigan on scholarship and kept asking Tie where this school was. *University of Illinois? University of Chicago?* Tie finally says it was Notre Dame."

Because he didn't play that often, Healey made a stop at the local library after the skate—this was before the Internet—for a little NCAA research. "That night, guys are all in their underwear getting dressed," McKay said. "And Glenn yells over, 'Hey, Tie, what's the name of that school again? What year was that?'"

"I told you, Notre Dame," Tie growled. "Around 1990."

Healey pulled out a piece of paper with his findings and said, "that's funny. There was no hockey program at Notre Dame that year."

"Tie chased Glenn all around that new Boston Garden, both of them pretty much naked," McKay said.

Domi would get his revenge whenever the Leafs would be going down a giant escalator at the airport or a hotel. He'd be at the front or the back of the line and press the stop button, triggering a full team stumble.

Donut Man

The Tim Hortons donut store near Buffalo's First Niagara Center has what every big outlet in the chain should: a statue of Horton outside. The Leafs and Buffalo Sabres star began with a small operation—after his attempt at a burger joint failed—that's become a worldwide fast food giant. In the early days, his enterprise was considered a lark until Punch Imlach tried to lowball the defenceman in a contract year. Horton responded by having a box of donuts delivered to Imlach to indicate he had the financial means to hold out. Imlach found the reply hilarious and eventually brought Horton to Buffalo when he took over the expansion Sabres in the early '70s.

Darryl Sittler received a sterling silver English tea service for his 10-point night. Ditto for defenceman Ian Turnbull after his record five-goal game by a defenceman on February 2, 1977. But when Rick Vaive became the first Toronto player to reach 50 goals in a season in 1981–82, getting all the way to 54, the Leafs owner was no longer in a giving mood. Vaive received nothing from Ballard for his feat or for hitting the 50 mark twice more before being traded. A local tavern got word of the slight after Vaive passed the milestone the first time and gave him 50 certificates for one free draft beer. Vaive and some thirsty teammates redeemed them all in one night.

Checking centre Jimmy Jones was in awe of Sittler from the moment he made the team in 1977–78. "Darryl was the epitome of heart and character," Jones said. "I have a vivid memory of one of the first pre-season games I played in, at London, Ontario. It didn't count in the standings, but when a teammate shot the puck down the ice, Darryl raced after it, skating full steam the length of the rink to avoid an icing call. He gave 100 percent whether the game counted or not."

Jones also saw why Sittler and right winger Lanny McDonald had such great chemistry. Each of them were small-town Canadians. Sittler was from St. Jacob's, Ontario, and McDonald was from Hanna, Alberta. "Lanny had gentlemanly good sportsmanship that never wavered, even in the most intense and heated matches," Jones said. "When the team was on a roll, Lanny could always be persuaded to sing 'Alberta Bound,' complete with foot stomping, hand clapping, and at least four notes off-key."

Jones also appreciated the roguish Tiger Williams for having his back and all those other Leafs who needed a bodyguard. Jones said Williams was a player "who made it to the NHL with sheer guts and will power." But Jones gradually learned he had to give Williams a little more space. "Tiger had a strange pregame ritual of breaking a hockey stick over a wooden bench in the centre of the dressing room," Jones said. "He also kept a set of boxing gloves in his stall and would spar with anyone who came walking in or out of the dressing room."

Meanwhile, Jones' partner on the Leafs' annoyingly effective checking line was winger Jerry Butler, who could chirp with the best of them. "Jerry's wise cracking rarely subsided even during a game," Jones said.

After a stoppage in play because fans threw some coins on the ice, Don Ashby, who was going through a divorce, skated over to pick up a loose dime. "Remember, your wife gets one half of that, too," Butler yelled out. And Jones said goalie Mike Palmateer came by his nickname,

"The Popcorn Kid," quite honestly. He really did devour a box of it before every game. "You couldn't walk near Mike's bench spot in the dressing room without hearing the crackling of popcorn kernels being crunched under foot," Jones said.

Jones went on to coach the Marlboro juniors and join the York Regional Police Force just north of the city.

* * *

When Ed Olczyk's wife, Diana, went into labour, her husband was with the Leafs. By the time baby Thomas was born at a Toronto-area hospital, Ed was a Winnipeg Jet. November 10, 1990 was certainly a wild day for the Olczyks, starting when Diana was admitted to the maternity ward. Ed called it "an eight out of 10" in terms of how close delivery time was. Then a nurse tapped him on the back. "There were no cell phones back then of course, so she hands me a note [from the Leafs]," Olczyk said in conversation with Sportsnet in 2018. "I told her, 'Just tell 'em I'll be at the game later tonight.' She goes away, comes back, and says, 'No, they really want to talk to you.' Diana is flat on her back, I've already got my catcher's mitt on, but I leave the delivery room to take the call from Bob Stellick. He first asked how Diana was doing. I said, 'I gotta go,' but he gives the phone to general manager Floyd Smith, who says, 'We hate to do this, but we just traded you to the Jets.' I go back in the room, and my wife says, 'Where the hell have you been'? I [lied] 'Umm, my aunt's sick.' But she just looked at me and said, 'Where are we going?'"

Not only did Diana's instincts correctly tell her a trade had gone down, but when Ed gave her a guess for their destination, she nailed Winnipeg on the first try. "It ended up being a great move because I loved The 'Peg," said Olczyk, who would have two tours of duty with the Jets as well as play for the '94 Stanley Cup champion New York Rangers, Mario Lemieux's Pittsburgh Penguins, and back where he started in his hometown of Chicago. Olczyk became one of the most well-known hockey analysts on American network television and survived a very public battle with colon cancer.

Olczyk's time in Toronto included two seasons as the Leafs' leading scorer, one of them a 42-goal campaign. He was the first American-born player to become a leading scorer on the team. But the trade to the Jets came after a sour start to the 1990–91 season, a difference of opinion with head coach Doug Carpenter, and significant public belief that he was too chummy with off-ice pal Gary Leeman to the detriment of team bonding. So when the Leafs floundered after his deal (they would not make the playoffs in '91), Olczyk didn't miss a chance to sound off the first time Toronto visited Winnipeg. "If people thought that [trade] was going to solve the problem, that the Leafs were suddenly going to go on to bigger and better things, then I guess the games have spoken for themselves," Olczyk said. "It's gone the other way. I've learned a lot from the situation, but nobody can ever take away what I accomplished in Toronto, what we did as a team, and what Gary and I had as a friendship. That's the kind of thing that bothered me the most—the perception. You hear it somewhere, and it's etched in stone. No one ever said anything about Daniel Marois and Vince Damphousse hanging around together. When you start to fix something that isn't broken, it ends up shattering, and that's what happened."

*   *   *

When Borje Salming came to Toronto for the announcement of his statue on Legends Row, he exchanged a big hug with Bob McGill. Some 25 years earlier, the two teammates had a much different kind of embrace in a game in Detroit. Salming had been accidentally sliced in the face by the skate of Red Wings forward Gerard Gallant while down in a crease mash-up. Salming was extremely lucky not to have had his career ended that night at Joe Louis Arena with loss of sight—or worse. Of all the injuries the Swede suffered in his 16 years as a Leaf, none was more horrific. The deep cut started on his temple, miraculously skirted his right eye, and wound down to the edge of his lip. As Salming staggered to the Toronto bench to stop the bleeding, McGill was there to catch the Swede before he passed out. "You know how someone [who] gets cut on the ice leaves a little path of blood drops to the bench?" McGill asked. "Well, this was a big red trail. And when they stitched him up, he looked like something from a monster movie."

Salming recalled no real pain from the actual skate making contact. "It was when the bandages came off," Salming said of the famous gruesome photo of the stitch job. "I thought I'd look like that the rest of my life."

Gallant was also shaken up by the incident. "I remember being in front of the net, trying to score and got a big shove from behind by their big guy, Chris Kotsopoulos," Gallant said. "I lost my balance, looked down, and the next thing I saw was blood gushing out."

He commended the Detroit medical staff for their tireless work on Salming throughout that evening. "Our doctor put all those stitches in him and did an unbelievable job because today he looks really good," Gallant said. "It was an awful thing, but there was no intent by me, and Borje has said that to me many times. In fact, a couple of years later, I went over to play in the world championships in Stockholm. There was a big article in the paper on Borje, talking about the injury and praising me as a player."

Salming was never formally named a Leafs captain. But few players in team history led by example as he did, had such a pioneering role as a European NHLer, was loved as much by fans in Toronto, and sparked so many stories. He was the grandson of a reindeer herder and son of a miner. His father's death at a young age prompted his mother to urge him to find a safer profession above ground. He was discovered by accident when the Leafs were scouting other countrymen.

Salming was a game star in his debut on October 10, 1973, a 7–4 win against Buffalo, and he had to be pushed back out on the ice as he was unfamiliar with the ritual. He was a natural athlete, having excelled at European handball before following older brother, Stig, into hockey.

"He could've been a pro tennis player, an auto racer, just about any-thing he wanted," teammate Jim McKenny told author Dave Shoalts.

If he saw some men playing chess in the park, he couldn't stop him-self from hanging over the game as an observer, then getting invited to take on the winner, and then usually winning himself. "He'd play two games at once and win," McKenny said.

Salming quickly became one of the boys, who could play hard on and off the ice. Steve Thomas recalled the day Salming proved himself to be Nordic through and through. "We were in Banff, Alberta, staying there during a break in a trip after playing Edmonton and before we went to Calgary," Thomas said. "We had a couple of days off, so we all decided to go skiing. We went and rented all the gear. Everything was perfect, and we went out and [invested in ski clothes], too. Now we're ready to go up to the mountain, and all of a sudden we see Borje. He's going down the slopes wearing just his tie, jacket, and overcoat—and skiing like a pro while doing it."

* * *

When Kerry Fraser worked his last regular-season game before retir-ing at age 57 in 2010, he chose it to be Toronto, where he'd begun in the '70s working an exhibition game between the Leafs and Montreal Canadiens. He believed one of the secrets to respect and longevity in an often heated game was keeping things light with team tough guys. In Toronto's case, that meant their two penalty minute kings, Williams and Domi. "[Enforcers] were most often the most respected on their team," Fraser said. "[In wild games] I'd go to Tiger and say, 'Enough's enough. I mean what I say,' and through that relationship, he would convey that message to his team."

Fraser even made peace with Pat Quinn, a notorious ref-baiter. Fraser laughed when recounting the night the New York Rangers hon-oured his 1,500th game in 2003 against the Leafs, and Quinn was spot-ted giving half-hearted applause at the bench. "One good game and

1,499 lousy ones" was Quinn's barb, but when the latter was in his sunset years coaching the Edmonton Oilers, and Fraser was on his farewell tour, the two had a warm postgame chat.

* * *

Domi started out with the Leafs as a high draft pick and a noted hothead who earned the nickname of the Albanian Assasin. But by the time he made his second coming with Toronto after his initial trade to the New York Rangers, he was a 26-year-old father of two, including future NHL first-round pick Max Domi. So when eager Oilers player Dennis Bonvie came off the bench in a 1995 game in Edmonton, looking to take on the league's heavyweight champ, Domi felt he had to oblige. But he added a message for Bonvie through his postgame comments. "The kid has to learn you have to play this game, as well as fight," Domi said. "It was funny to watch him come over and start talking to me because I was just like him when I started."

Domi had exchanged a lot of punches the night before with Vancouver Canucks player Gino Odjick, someone he truly had a long history with, so he was not really interested in Bonvie. But their meeting was built up like a prize fight in the Edmonton papers, as Bonvie was in a battle with Louie DeBrusk to be the team's policeman. "It was an unfair situation for Tie," noted fellow enforcer Ken Baumgartner.

Domi lectured Bonvie that DeBrusk was a fine example in his own room to emulate.

"Louie's a player, he can skate," said Domi, who had a goal that night to underline his value to the Leafs. "But I guess they're having trouble selling tickets here."

At 6:59 of the second period, Bonvie was given his chance, gleefully coming over the boards and starting to jabber at Domi from 15 feet away. "He said, 'Don Cherry wants to see this,'" Domi said, laughing. "That broke me up."

They fought to a draw. Bonvie later worked for the Leafs as a scout in the Brian Burke era. "My first fight was with Kevin McClelland," Domi said. "I must have said something, but I don't remember. Too many punches in the head over the years."

When Domi sucker-punched Ulf Samuelsson of the Rangers at the Gardens, it was said that at least one NHLer on another team rose in applause when he saw it on TV—happy that the rogue Swede was finally faced frontier justice. Fans in Boston, who loathed Samuelson for a hit that damaged Cam Neely's knee, likely didn't mind either.

But Domi was slapped with an eight-game suspension for the mild concussion and seven-stitch cut to Samuelsson and $25,000 fine, something that was a lot more painful to the wallet back in 1995. He claimed for years that Samuelsson was mocking him as "Tie Dummy" that night and challenging him to drop the gloves. "I'm glad Ulf's not [seriously] hurt," Domi said later. "Maybe I shouldn't have done what I did. It was reaction, spur of the moment. He said, 'C'mon, Dummy, let's fight' three times. We were down 2–0, and he was rubbing my face in it."

The New York Times suggested Domi might have misunderstood Samuelsson's accent and thought he heard "dummy" instead of "Domi." "I prayed to God he didn't break Samuelsson's jaw or he would've got 30 games," said Burke, the then-NHL senior vice president who was watching the fight on TV at the time.

Nik Antropov joined the ranks of Leafs who made enforcer Domi the target of their practical jokes. "My first year, I didn't speak any English. I didn't understand any," Antropov said. "So I don't know why I decided to pull a prank on Tie. I cut down his sticks so they'd break at one of those Leaf skills competitions. But somebody ratted me out. Next day, we were practising at Lakeshore Lions, and I was late getting back in the room because I was a rookie and had to stay out late for extra skating. I came in, and all my clothes were in the hot tub."

Thomas also enjoyed a joke at Domi's expense. "We'd cut one leg off one of his dress pants and make him walk through an airport like that," he said.

*   *   *

Referee Ron Wicks, a Sudbury native, enjoyed living in the Greater Toronto Area with many other officials, though he knew it would bring him into some potentially controversial games involving the Leafs. One such match was March 12, 1984 at the Gardens versus the Jets. The Leafs messed up a huge lead and lost 8–7 on a hotly debated Paul MacLean overtime goal. Toronto captain Vaive immediately argued it was kicked in, but Wicks and linesman Leon Stickle let it stand. According to Wicks, Vaive menacingly stuck his blade between Stickle's legs and received a warning that may or may not have included bodily harm from all the zebras if the Leafs winger raised it any further.

Dave Hutchison, the huge Leafs enforcer, then continued some verbal jousting with the crew before stalking away. After Stickle drove Wicks home, the latter's wife was waiting for him. She was upset a Toronto TV sportscaster had lampooned Wicks' work, which prompted a crank phone call to the house, berating her husband as "a [bleeping] asshole." "It was not easy being an impartial arbitrator in Leafs Nation," Wicks later wrote in his autobiography. "And all this crap took place because the Leafs had snatched defeat from the jaws of victory once again."

The late Wicks and his younger brother Jim, a fervent Leafs fan, always ribbed each other about the team's fortunes and Ron's supposed bias against them. Ron zinged him one day with this: "What do they call a Maple Leafs player holding the Stanley Cup? A visitor to the Hockey Hall of Fame."

*   *   *

Some of the best Leafs tales originated around Christmas. In 1968, when clubs still played on December 24 or 25, the team bus was going through the near-deserted South Side of Chicago. Having lost the last game in Detroit and forced to miss Christmas Eve in Toronto, there was a lot of "bah humbug" aboard. Suddenly a baritone voice at the back started belting out carols. All eyes glared at the offender, rookie defenceman Quinn. He later said he just couldn't stop himself from getting in the spirit of the day. "Tim Horton, Dave Keon—the veterans are all staring at me. That kind of thing just wasn't done," he said. "But by the end, a few of them were singing along with me."

The Leafs beat the Chicago Blackhawks 4–3.

A couple of years before Quinn did his Bing Crosby imitation, the authoritarian Imlach showed some festive spirit, too. He granted his farmhand son, Brent, his third and final NHL game as an injury stopgap in a Christmas Eve/Christmas Day home-and-home sweep of Boston. And because the Leafs and Bruins couldn't fly out after the match on Christmas Eve due to bad weather on the eastern seaboard, the teams bused to Buffalo to catch a train, arriving at 2:30 PM. The senior Imlach didn't mind the delays. "Those kids in Boston got to have snow for Christmas and that's what I'm giving them," he joked.

We stirred the pot a little one year by asking Finnish defenceman Jyrki Lumme and Swedish winger Jonas Hoglund which Nordic nation is the true home to Santa Claus. "Of course Santa is Finnish," Lumme said, almost insulted by the question. "He is called *Joulupukki*. He has a big centre in Korvatunturi."

"Santa could never be Finnish," Hoglund replied of Scandinavia's *Jultomte*. "He's too nice a guy."

Russian Alex Mogilny said he grew up wary of the whole Santa myth in the bad old days of the Soviet Union. "Does he live in the north?" Mogilny asked. "I don't know where the hell he lives, really. They never told us. Maybe he's in one of those government project buildings. But he comes from somewhere."

As kids the Leafs received all manner of holiday presents—not all themed on hockey.

"I would always get a stick, but there was a bike I got when I was about eight years old," said Auston Matthews. "I still rode it up until

[2014]. Not a mountain bike, just a regular bike, black and grey colours. Never broke down on me. All my buddies had one, too. It's still in my garage. You could still ride it today, though I choose not to."

"I got a Schwinn bike, when I was about 10 years old," defenceman Morgan Rielly added. "My dad rolled them in the house Christmas Day, and that was a big one for us. Mine was black and red, and my brother had one [in] blue and white. Schwinn makes racing bikes, too, but mine was a mountain bike, my first one that ever had shocks. I took it up to Whistler and ride it down. That was the present that gave me the most memories, and that's how you have to file your Christmas gifts."

The late Wade Belak hoped to have Appaloosa show horses like his father in rural Saskatchewan, but the family had to sell some of theirs to put Wade and his brother through hockey. "To buy another one was out of the question," Belak said in the early 2000s. "It was [a big sacrifice], and you appreciated it."

Corey Schwab, who played goal in 2001–02, received his first set of pads at age seven. They were used ones from the local minor hockey association in North Battleford, Saskatchewan. "I was all set in my Ski-Doo suit on the steps, hoping for my two older brothers to come home and shoot on me," Schwab said. "My parents have a picture of me in my stuff, falling asleep on the step as I waited. When I was older, my brother Darin gave me a plain, white [Jason Voorhees]-style goalie mask. He must have got it from a catalogue. I put stickers from the Saskatoon Blades, my favourite team, all over it."

Centre Alyn McCauley was constantly disappointed when his request for goalie pads under the tree were dashed. "I'd taken them off of my list when my grandparents surprised me with a pair," he said. "I played one game in novice and was scored on 12 times. If I stayed with goaltending, I don't think I would be in [the NHL]."

Computer games, *Don Cherry's Rock 'Em Sock 'Em* fighting videos, and bubble table hockey games were popular with the most recent generation of Leafs, but half the fun was trying to guess what gifts parents had purchased. "I was about 13 or 14, checking out the wrapped presents under the tree," Lumme said. "There was one addressed to me that I just couldn't figure out. It was like a heavy tube, and all day I poked it, shook it, tried to feel through the paper, but I couldn't guess. It turned out to be a dumbbell."

Curiosity got the better of winger Garry Valk. "I really wanted a Gretzky Titan hockey stick. I went looking around the garage just before Christmas and found where my parents had hidden it," Valk said. "I was dreaming all about what I'd do with it, but when they found out I'd been snooping, they wouldn't give it to me for a few days to teach me a lesson."

In Russia, New Year's was a bigger deal than Christmas. Mogilny recalled a low-key exchange of gifts and a high capacity of alcohol consumption. "You put presents under the tree," he said, "and hopefully by the time you [sober] up the next evening, something is still there. The best one I ever got was a nice orange."

*   *   *

One of the most uncomfortable—and unusual—Leafs team pictures took place at the Gardens in the late 1980s. This job fell to Graig Abel, who looked at the annual assignment with a mixture of pride and dread. The seating arrangement—rows of execs, coaches, and players—had to be approved by Harold Ballard, who at the time owned a lively dog, a big Bouvier des Flandres named TC Puck. The dog had the run of the building and sometimes disrupted practice as he went back and forth behind the bench and through the seats behind the net, barking loudly and trying to chase the players.

Ballard saw nothing wrong with TC's antics and didn't care that his coaches were distracted from conducting practice. He considered TC the team's official mascot and ordered he should sit by him right at the front of the photo. TC sat quietly at centre ice for the first couple of frames but then began to yowl and wouldn't stop. Ballard was shouting at him to "sit nice," but it was his partner, Yolanda, who noticed the freshly groomed ice was not the best thing for TC's exposed genitals. "Hey, Harold, the dog's balls are sticking to the ice," Yolanda shouted from the sidelines.

The players couldn't keep a straight face as Ballard fought to keep TC quiet and sitting still, while Abel kept shooting "the goofiest picture I've ever taken."

* * *

Pregame rituals went a long way back in the NHL, and Shayne Corson was no different.

"For me, we would always leave the room at the same time and we had our funny little thing, tapping someone or something," Corson said. "And the Leafs still do that. When I watch the games, and the [video

Known for his aggressiveness, Shayne Corson fights with Clarke Wilm of the Calgary Flames in 2002.

board] shows the things they do, the high-fiving. I tried to be the last guy or the second last guy out. And I tried to leave the warm-up last, no matter who we played. Unfortunately, when I was with Montreal, we threw the puck in the empty net in Philadelphia, and there was the big brawl."

Corson was referring to the NHL's last full-scale, bench-clearing melee during Game 6 of the 1987 Eastern Conference Final. Teammate Claude Lemieux—like Corson, a noted troublemaker—was also fanatical about being last off the ice at warm-up and scoring in the opponent's empty cage on his way to the gate.

The Philadelphia Flyers had grown incensed with Lemieux's bold act as the hard-fought series wore on, especially with the game in question at the Spectrum. Ed "Boxcar" Hospodar, one of the last vintage Broad Street Bullies, gave Lemieux a direct warning not to attempt his empty netter. Lemieux appeared to comply, so the Flyers left the ice, but Lemieux and Corson snuck back out to try and repeat their ritual before the Zamboni came out. Hospodar and backup goalie Chico Resch caught them and charged out after the two Habs, and all players—in various stages of dress—stormed from each dressing room into the trenches. There were no referees or linesmen to intercede. Figuring Lemieux would trigger something before the game, the Flyers supposedly had 24 players in uniform for the pregame skate to Montreal's 18 skaters and two goalies. "That night was the craziest," Corson said.

The NHL legislated such donnybrooks out of the game that year.

One of Corson's last duels was as a Leafs player with journeyman Steve Webb of the New York Islanders in Game 6 of the 2002 playoffs. Webb had truly rattled the Leafs, but the 5–3 New York win ended with he and Corson uttering threats at each other from the end of their opposing benches. "Steve did his job. He was great at what he did. He drove me crazy on the ice," Corson said. "In the heat of that moment, I didn't say very nice things to him. It was along the lines of 'I'm going to kill you.'"

* * *

For the most part, medical staff, trainers, and equipment men on rival teams cooperate to make sure game preparation and the match itself proceed smoothly. If the Leafs are short some gear, need a patch job, or if the visitors' sweaters need to be washed for another road game, it's all good, and the courtesy is reciprocated as the season progresses. But playoffs are a different matter. As soon as the Leafs circle the postseason dates, they circle the wagons to make doubly sure there is no funny business from the opposition. "Basically, you don't take chances," one-time athletic therapist Brent Smith said. "On the road we take along our own doctors, a dentist, and lots of extra medical supplies so we don't have to borrow anything from another team."

St. Louis' rink proved problematic for the Leafs in 1996. Toronto arrived in the midwest spring heat for its practice and found their Kiel Center quarters unbearably hot and had to bring in its own air conditioning unit. Injuring his knee during the series, Mats Sundin required a specially ordered brace be flown in from out of town. It was delivered to the Blues' room by mistake in the morning and was kept there all day until finally being passed on to the Leafs near faceoff time of an elimination game. Despite a brave effort by Sundin playing at far less than 100 percent, the Leafs lost the match and the series. Later, Quinn had his suspicions that the Blues doctored the ice to slow it down whenever the swifter Leafs visited.

Scotty Bowman liked to time a paint job for the visitors' room at Detroit's Joe Louis Arena for when playoff foes arrived. But while Toronto had to contend with the fumes on a couple of regular-season game nights, the two old rivals did not meet in postseason action during Bowman's reign.

* * *

Getting inside an NHL team's weight room/meeting room is next to impossible under stricter access rules these days. But Islanders general manager Mike Milbury invited a group of his beat writers and Toronto's to come inside the Nassau Coliseum enclave in the '02 playoffs. He had a little TV show he wanted to share.

Tired of Quinn dominating air time about a perceived imbalance of penalties in their bitter series despite the Leafs' 2–0 lead, Milbury appeared at the end of coach Peter Laviolette's press conference with a video tape and motioned to a select group of reporters to follow him.

Inside the Isles' weight room, Milbury broke down Game 1 and 2 highlights like they were the Zapruder film. He showed his audience what he called flagrant fouls by the Leafs, a Corson spear, a Sundin trip, and worst of all, ex-Islander Bryan McCabe's infamous can opener, where the defenceman jammed his stick into the blades of an oncoming opponent, making him susceptible to being easily knocked off his feet.

All the while, Milbury was supplying incendiary commentary, punctuated with f-bombs.

"That's a eff-ing penalty," he shouted at the TV as he watched McCabe. "You can not put your stick between a guy's legs. It's an illegal play. He did it when he was here and he shouldn't get away with it. We've been trying to get that out for years. We put it in the rule book because of that."

Milbury also used the clips to show the referees were in full view of the transgressions and even ran the live feed from *Hockey Night in Canada* as analyst Harry Neale described the can opener as McCabe's "signature move." "Signature move," Milbury hissed. "It's eff-ing illegal, it's an eff-ing penalty. He can't eff-ing pivot that well. That's why he uses it."

Naturally, Milbury's diatribe made all the headlines the next day. Though he ended the session by saying the officials had a tough job, the league socked him with a $30,000 fine.

But it had the desired effect. McCabe's controversial move was penalized by the officials the next night, and he was also called for impeding Shawn Bates on a breakaway, leading to a penalty shot goal and a second Toronto loss to tie the set.

Wild Bunch

Freed from Imlach's vise-like grip on their lives, the early '70s Leafs were a team of Good-Time Charlies. They loved to hoist a pint and stay out late, which didn't sit well with goaltender Jacques Plante. "Plante would squeal on us a lot for drinking," said Jim McKenny, one of the most notorious of the wild bunch at the time. "But John McLellan, our coach, would say, 'I know they're drinking, Jacques. Tell me some real news.' John just didn't want any empty bottles rattling around the dressing room."

The NHL Players Association called a strike to begin April 1, 1992, in a battle over revenue with the league that included which side should profit from hockey card sales. While the work stoppage was fully forecast days earlier, the Islanders were still obligated to fly to Toronto for a game scheduled just after the strike deadline. The Isles showed up, took a few morning spins around the ice, and went to lunch. "We tried to make it business as usual right down to the pregame meal," said former Leafs player Tom Kurvers, who became the Isles' player rep. "Some guys still wanted to take a pregame nap."

When the strike officially began at 3:00 PM, Kurvers had to get out the American Express card issued to him by the union to buy the team one-way tickets home that night. A few Isles living in the Toronto area just stayed put for the duration.

The strike ruined plans for the Leafs to salute Ace Bailey, a star in the 1930s whose career was ended by a blind-side attack from the much-feared Eddie Shore of the Boston Bruins. After many of the club's greats were shunned in the Ballard era, the Leafs were set to hoist retired No. 6 and 5 banners for Bailey and Bill Barilko, respectively, the night of the game against the Isles.

The 88-year-old Bailey, who was on the first Leafs and Gardens Cup team in 1932, was really looking forward to the ceremony and a private limousine the club arranged for him.

Sadly, Bailey died a week later before the strike ended and games resumed.

Another casualty of the short-lived strike was career minor leaguer Mike MacWilliam, who was called up by the Leafs the week of the labour dispute. MacWilliam, who would rack up 301 penalty minutes that season with the AHL St. John's Leafs, was not needed once the dispute ended. His first and only NHL action came a few years later, ironically as a member of the Isles.

* * *

Wendel Clark took Leafs Nation by storm in the 1985–86 season, and it started on June draft day at the Metro Toronto Convention Centre. It was to be the first NHL draft to be televised live by the Canadian Broadcasting Corporation, and media-savvy assistant GM Gord Stellick wanted to make sure his club's big moment had national exposure. He had a carefully rehearsed plan with Clark and agent Don Meehan to hand Clark his sweater in the stands at the same moment he was announced by GM Gerry McNamara.

Clark's name brought the intended hearty applause, but just as Stellick reached him with the neatly folded jersey, a shoulder block from either the CBC's Don Wittman or one of the camera crew boxed Stellick right out of the picture. Clark's interview during his slow walk toward the Leafs table proceeded without the main prop carried by a glum-looking Stellick in the background. But when Clark neared the Leafs table, Stellick found his nerve and told him to pause and exchange his suit jacket for the dark blue Toronto jersey. As it slid over his shoulders and his head popped out, a louder cheer rolled through the ballroom to the relief of Stellick.

The quiet youngster from Kelvington, Saskatchewan, could score but also used his hands as weapons of mass destruction against foes who tried to pick on the Leafs. With the Leafs serving as doormats for a few years, fans seized on Clark as a lightning rod for positive change. "He gave us credibility on and off the ice," Bob Stellick said. "He became a big part of Toronto, but he never lost the Kelvington in him. That first year, whatever the goals meant, people remember the fights. He'd take on guys such as Behn Wilson. I'll always remember director of officiating John McCauley noting that, after he fought he'd skate right by the other team's bench, and it was quiet. No one chirped him.

"It was an era when people enjoyed fights that weren't staged. There weren't 240-pound guys calling each other at the hotel on game day to say, 'I need more fights [for a new contract]' and thanking each other later. Wendel didn't thank anyone at the end of his fights. It was to the death. Usually, his first punch hit you before his glove hit the ice. He was 5'11" and knew he had to get his shots in really quick."

One of the heaviest hits Clark leveled was the bowling ball check on defenceman Bruce Bell of the Blues during the 1986–87 season. It frequently shows up in videos as one of the 10 hardest jolts of all time, a list that will not be extended very long now that such checks are infrequent or monitored closely by the league. At any rate, Clark came in unseen as Bell, whose head was down, collected the puck behind his net and was knocked cold with a shoulder-to-chest shot. There was a predictable response from the Blues, who sent a couple of their bigger players after Clark, while the Leafs tried to hold them off and allow for a St. Louis trainer to attend to Bell.

* * *

John Kordic was one of those players who had a spicy quote morning, noon, and night—whether you needed one or not. Most knew he was a bit of a loose cannon when he arrived via trade with the Canadiens on November 8, 1988. In one game against Buffalo—after he'd taken down one of the tougher Sabres—a follically-challenged member of Buffalo's staff was among those haranguing Kordic from the bench as the linesmen escorted him past. Noting the guy's toupee, Kordic snapped, "next time your cat dies, don't put it on your head."

But Kordic's sense of humour afforded him scant moments of levity in his time as a Leafs player. During a team dinner at Joe Forte's in Vancouver, he got into it with mild-mannered goalie Allan Bester and slapped him across the face hard enough to knock his glasses off. A patron witnessed the incident and called the local papers, spreading word early enough that Leafs writers, who were scattered around Vancouver, had to be located by their offices and quickly piece together details for the 2:00 AM final editions.

Kordic arrived here in exchange for handsome and flashy forward Russ Courtnall, who was quite popular with fans but less so with his coaches. When John Brophy was in charge, he busted the light-hitting Courtnall down to the fourth line, prompting the latter's trade request. Brophy's fatal attempt to put as many heavyweights in the lineup as possible steered Stellick to trigger the Courtnall-for-Kordic deal. The move made some sense at the time to help Courtnall get a fresh start on a more skill-oriented team and to bring in someone to give the Leafs more backbone in the "Chuck" Norris Division.

But Kordic also came with a litany of personal problems. He'd feuded in Montreal with Burns, who'd fought fire with fire and allegedly threw an ashtray at Kordic's head during a heated argument in the coach's office. The loss of their beloved Courtnall for the rough-hewn Kordic went over poorly with Leafs fans when no appreciable difference in team fortunes followed. The trade became a sleek jet exchanged for a plane wreck. "People were obsessed about Kordic-Courtnall," Stellick said. "It was definitely my Bob Uecker moment, the one boner they still talk about."

Given a do-over of the deal, Stellick said he'd have still opted for the trade but one that would've sent Courtnall to a market far less visible. "When Imlach traded Lanny McDonald to Colorado, Lanny went right out of sight," Stellick said. "Unfortunately for me, it seemed Russ was on TV every Saturday in Montreal with his perfect teeth and scoring four goals a night, even though he only had 22 for them that year. He was a sexy player, but when you tuned in to Kordic, it was like an episode of that show, *Cops*."

Kordic was soon suspended 10 games for an unprovoked stick attack on Edmonton's Keith Acton, a player half his size. The incident came after Brophy had slammed Kordic's effort between periods of the game in front of the entire team, which had the negative effect of prodding Kordic to be even more reckless. The time serving that suspension is when many believe Kordic fell in with the wrong crowd, adding to an aggressive nature linked to suspected steroid use. The death of Kordic's father from cancer around the same time, a man whom he knew had come to detest his playing style, contributed to his fragmented mental state.

At one point, an AWOL Kordic was found, drowning his sorrows by two Toronto writers at a bar right across the street from the Gardens. Carpenter, Brophy's successor, tried to reform him—but to no avail. The Leafs traded him to the Washington Capitals, where a further downward spiral of off-ice issues and failed rehab efforts eventually led him to Quebec City and an aborted tryout with the Nordiques. It was there at a seedy motel that several police got into a fight to subdue the strung out Kordic. He died in the ambulance of heart failure.

The Leafs have kept themselves largely out of the performance-enhancing drugs saga. But in the days after he played in Toronto and before becoming its coach, Randy Carlyle was caught up in one the dopiest doping allegations ever. It was at the 1989 world championships in Stockholm after Canada's 8–2 win against West Germany that Caryle was randomly asked for a urine sample, and a flood of trouble ensued. Carlyle, then a defenceman with the Jets, tested positive for the anabolic steroid, mesterolone. Reaction among teammates at first was that someone had pulled an elaborate practical joke. A tad pudgy late in his playing career, the 33-year-old defenceman hardly fit the steroid-abuser profile. "When we heard the words 'steroids' and 'Randy' in the same sentence, everyone in the room laughed," recalled Dave Ellett, Carlyle's teammate and later a member of the Leafs. "It was John Ferguson Sr., who had the best line of all: 'if that's what steroids does for your body, a lot of people will want their money back.' Then we realized how serious it was. It could cost us at the tournament, and Randy would be suspended. Back in Winnipeg there was media all around Randy's house, and his family was going through a lot of trauma."

Rather than suspect the Soviets, who had a reputation for underhanded tactics, Alan Eagleson and the Canadian delegation believed the host nation had some explaining to do. It was their test facility, and there was a big Canada-Sweden game coming up that Carlyle would miss.

Mesterolone at the time was available only in Sweden and used primarily in the treatment of breast malignancy, torn muscles, and sex-change operations.

Carlyle had been sequestered in the hotel from the crush of media from all countries looking for comment. It was believed he'd be sent home the moment his B sample test results came back, as they almost always mirrored the A. An international and possibly NHL ban was feared. Very early that morning, I was summoned, along with Frank Orr of the *Toronto Star*, William Houston of *The Globe and Mail*, and the late Geoff Fraser of *The Canadian Press*, to Eagleson's suite. The Eagle had brought out the heavyweights: Canadian ambassador to Sweden Dennis Browne and visiting Canadian Supreme Court Justice John Sopinka. Before his fall from power, Eagleson knew how to show he wouldn't be intimidated in a road game. "All the right people are in this room to declare war on Sweden," Orr whispered to me.

Eagleson then stunned the room by reporting the B sample was negative and then produced a relieved Carlyle from his hiding place in another room. "A one-in-a-million chance," Eagleson said of the B result and the resolution, though Orr couldn't resist a jab. "Eagle, the last time a miracle like this happened," he said, "three Wise Men came from the East."

A lot of people were left shaking their heads. "It could have been someone contaminated the urine or it could've been bad test equipment," Team Canada doctor Charles Bull said. "The chances that Randy's drink was spiked are small. They would've had to spike all 22 players that game."

Carlyle only recalled taking an anti-inflammatory tablet for the tourney for a sore shoulder and a Vitamin B injection 18 months earlier. The International Ice Hockey Foundation (IIHF) medical commission could not account for the discrepancy in the testing. "There are one of 25 possible explanations," a commission official said. "There was a 1 percent chance that the A sample wouldn't be confirmed. I can't say it was a mistake. But it happens."

Given his chance to unload, Carlyle went after the IIHF. "I think this whole drug testing thing is horseshit," he said. "No player should have to go through it. I lost a lot of sleep, a few pounds through sweaty palms, and had a few bad dreams. It's unbelievable. How do you live with yourself, when across the world, people figure there was a foreign substance in your system?"

*   *   *

Lou Lamoriello was a father figure to Brendan Shanahan, whose own dad, Donal, had suffered from Alzheimer's disease and was not cognizant of his son's draft success. "I was in a rush," Brendan said of being picked third overall from the London Knights in 1987 by the New Jersey Devils, "in a mad dash to make it to the NHL. I made it when I was 18 years old, but it was too late. [Donal] was alive, but he wasn't with me."

The elder Shanahan, a Toronto fireman, attended the draft in Detroit in '87 and was often steered toward the TV by other family members when Brendan was being interviewed postgame. Yet sometimes he did not recognize his youngest son. Donal passed in 1990, Brendan's third season in the league, but his grave site was one of the first places the younger Shanahan brought the Cup when he won it with Detroit in 1997. He once confided to Lamoriello his doubts about his ability to play in the NHL as a teenager. "Brendan, I've been around in hockey a long time, and trust me, you have what it takes," Shanahan recalled the much older Lamoriello saying. "He was too good to send back to junior and yet he wasn't quite ready for the NHL," Lamoriello added. "It was a very difficult year for him. In hindsight, it maybe even made him a better power forward because he took it upon himself to get into the lineup by fighting. To see him become the player he became is just a pleasure."

A very different tone was evident in 2009, when a 40-year-old Shanahan approached Lamoriello for one more shot with the Devils at their 2009 training camp. He'd become the first NHLer to get 600 goals and 2,000 penalty minutes, but Lamoriello had to let him down—with a dash of humour. He said, "Brendan, I've been around in hockey a long time, and trust me, you no longer have what it takes."

ACKNOWLEDGMENTS

My gratitude to Bill Ames of Triumph Books for approaching me with this project. It brought back some great memories of more than 30-plus seasons on the Leafs beat. Much appreciation to Jeff Fedotin for editing this monster.

Thanks to all present and former Leafs players, coaches, executives, and team media people, who shared various stories with me for the *Toronto Sun* and this book in particular. A special stick tap to Gardens era friends Bob and Gord Stellick, Pat Park, Joe Bowen, Jim McKenny, Wayne Gillespie, and Mark Osborne for the foreword. Leafs historians Mike Wilson, Deb Thuet, and Paul Patskou have always provided invaluable resources to me without hesitation. My *Sun/Postmedia* family have been very supportive through the years for all my book projects, allowing me to think outside of the box for stories, features, and charts in the paper and giving promotional help. Thanks to my editors: Bill Pierce, Scott Morrison, Wayne Parrish, Dave Fuller, Pat Grier, John Iaboni, Mike Simpson, and the late, great Baron George Gross. Also to my longtime travelling beat partners: Paul Hunter, Kevin McGran, Gary Loewen, Frank Orr, and Dave Shoalts, who were part of many tales included in these pages.

No one in this line of work survives without incredible support on the home front, and my wife, Julie, and kids, Dylan and Kate, have always been patient when I keep saying "just five more minutes" at the computer.

SOURCES

Amodeo, Jim—*Bob Goldham Outside the Goal Crease*, 2018

Clark, Wendel—*Bleeding Blue*, Simon and Schuster, 2016

Conacher, Brian—*As the Puck Turns*, Wiley, 2007

Imlach, Punch—*Heaven and Hell in the NHL*, McLelland & Stewart, 1982

Kelly, Red—*The Red Kelly Story*, ECW Press, 2016

Shea, Kevin—*Diary of a Dynasty*, Firefly, 2010

Shoalts, Dave—*Tales from the Maple Leafs*, Sports Publishing, 2007

Stellick, Gord—*Hockey, Heartaches, and Hal*, Prentice Hall, 1990

Zweig, Eric—*The Toronto Maple Leafs, The Complete Oral History*, Dundurn 2017